The Journal of the Watcher

comeandreason
MINISTRIES

LENNOX
PUBLISHING

The Journal Of The Watcher is Published by Come and Reason Ministries

Author: Timothy R. Jennings

Illustrator: Louis Johnson

Edited by: Charles Mills

Copy Edited by: Claire VanderVelde

Copyright © 2015 Timothy R. Jennings and Louis Johnson. All rights reserved.

Come And Reason Ministries, PO Box 28266 Chattanooga, TN 37424

www.comeandreason.com

email: requests@comeandreason.com

ISBN: 978-0-9858502-5-8

All rights reserved. No part of this book may be reproduced or transmitted in any form or by any means, electronic or mechanical, including photocopying, recording, or by an information storage and retrieval system - except by a reviewer who may quote brief passages in a review to be printed in an online review, printed magazine or newspaper - without permission in writing from the publisher.

Table Of Contents

Intro - Prologue
Chapter One .... The Beginning Watch
Chapter Two .... War
Chapter Three .... Earth
Chapter Four .... Humanity
Chapter Five .... From Love to Fear
Chapter Six .... The Promise
Chapter Seven .... Earth's Early Skirmishes
Chapter Eight .... A Family from Ur
Chapter Nine .... A Little Theater
Chapter Ten .... The Distortion
Chapter Eleven .... Captivity
Chapter Twelve .... The Promised One
Chapter Thirteen .... Ministry
Chapter Fourteen .... Teaching
Chapter Fifteen .... Bread of Heaven
Chapter Sixteen .... Healing
Chapter Seventeen .... Truth Revealed
Chapter Eighteen .... Supper
Chapter Nineteen .... The Betrayal
Chapter Twenty .... The Trial
Chapter Twenty-One................... The Achievement
Chapter Twenty-Two .... The Victory
Chapter Twenty-Three .... The Future End

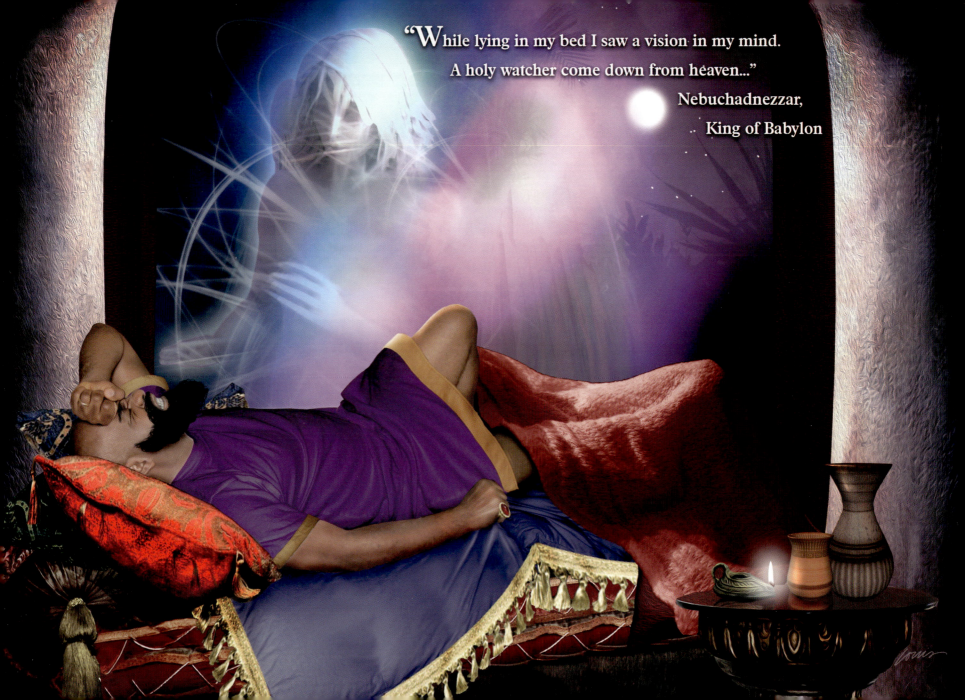

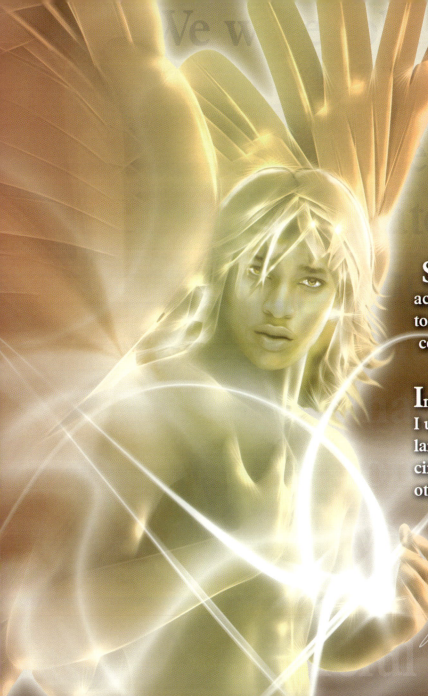

We were told by the Creator this day would come, the day Earth would need to know what we have observed. I am one of the Celestial Watchers. If you haven't heard of my kind, don't worry, most haven't. Unfortunately, many people on your planet haven't paid attention, and we have continued to watch unobserved. For well over 6,000 years we have watched, standing unnoticed, keeping careful record of all we have seen.

So now the time is right, and many of you will understand our account. The journal you hold in your hands began back very close to the beginning of all things. I have organized this journal to correspond with events from your planet's history.

In order to make my notes useful to the greatest number of people, I used a book on your planet that has been translated into more languages than any other and has more than six billion copies in circulation. Get a copy of this book. Some call it The Holy Oracles, others the Scriptures, but many know it as the Bible. I have correlated my observations with it, noting the converging points throughout. You will even see that several thousand years ago, a man named Daniel was given insight to a dream, revealing some of our activities to the king of Babylon. The event is written in his account in chapter 4 verses 13-23.

This journal chronicles the war that broke out in heaven, as beings of light began casting shadows, and as a planet teeming with life rebelled and became infected with death. We watched in horror as evil grew strong and millions died. I remember the dark days when hope itself seemed lost. But light broke through the darkness, yet the darkness fought and still fights to obstruct the light.

Soon the war between light and darkness will come to an end. However, you, and all who will listen, must be briefed on all that has transpired. The final conflict will be unimaginably severe and only those who are prepared - who know what's really going on - will survive. So it is the time for the Watchers to share the secrets we've observed; the vital back story that the darkness has tried to obstruct. This is necessary so that everyone on your planet will be ready for what's to come.

Our journey begins before your time was time. Before any creature or even the universe existed, in the beginning there was God: Father, Son, and Holy Spirit, a triune perfection of love and unity. Jesus - God's very thoughts made audible and visible - was with God. And Jesus was God. He was with God before anything else existed.

Together, they planned, designed, and engineered all future works of creation.

Jesus was the member of this triune perfection of love through whom everything was created. Without Jesus, nothing was created that has been created. (John 1:1-3, 17:24; Proverbs 8:23-30; Colossians 1:16-20)

As God created, He designed and engineered all things to operate in harmony with His own character of love. He built the universe to run upon the principle of love, the principle of other-centered giving, the principle of beneficence. This circle of never-ending giving is the basis on which the triune God created all life to operate. The circle of love is the foundation of life and is seen in everything God has made, because God is love and through Him all things hold together.
(1 John 4:8; 1 Corinthians 13:4; Romans 1:20; Colossians 1:17)

Jesus is the physical manifestation of the invisible God - the first being with physical form and the conduit from which all creation flows. He created everything: the entire universe, the heavens and the galaxies, angels, intelligent life, and all things visible and invisible. Authority and power stem from Him. Everything that exists was created by Him, for He existed before anything. It's Jesus who holds all things together. (Colossians 1:15-17; Proverbs 8:23-30)

The first sentient being Jesus created was the sum total of perfection, beauty, and intelligence. This being radiated the glory of God and became the template for subsequent manifestations of His creative power. Thus, at the dawn of creation, he was called "The Son of the Dawn," or Lucifer. Lucifer was absolutely perfect when he was made by Jesus. He was full of wisdom, exquisite in every detail, faultless, and excellent in every way. Lucifer loved Jesus and faithfully practiced the methods of love.
(Ezekiel 28:11-15; Isaiah 14:12)

God continued to create and bring forth more intelligent beings of various types: all perfect, all living in one accord, all existing in harmony with God's methods of love.
(Job 1:6, 38:7; Isaiah 6:2; 1 Corinthians 4:9; Ephesians 6:12; Colossians 1:16)

Lucifer was the most exalted of all the created beings, the angel appointed to stand in the very presence of God. He walked among the fiery stones of God's goodness and was privileged to receive wisdom directly from his creator and spread the light of truth about Him throughout the universe. But rather than growing in love, he instead freely chose to pervert himself with selfishness and pride. He became infatuated with self and loved his own beauty. His mind became warped, and he no longer loved others or valued truth.
(Ezekiel 28:14-17)

Lucifer deceived himself and thought his talents, beauty, ability, position, intelligence, and authority were innately his own. He forgot that all he possessed was a gift from God. He looked to himself and said, "I am as good as Jesus; I will exalt myself above Him. I will enthrone myself above the Creator in the minds and hearts of all intelligent creatures. I will be the one most loved, esteemed, and trusted. I will ascend to the highest pinnacle of popularity and affection, and displace God Himself as the one most loved and trusted in the universe." (Isaiah 14:12-14)

So Lucifer, the light-bearer of truth, perverted himself and exchanged the methods of love and truth for selfishness and lies. He left God's presence and spread falsehoods about Him throughout the heavens. He sowed seeds of discord and misrepresented long-known facts. He worked in secrecy and used flattery to mislead. He confused the angels and brought conflict to heaven. Lucifer, the covering cherub, corrupted his own mind and disqualified himself from being the guardian of love and truth. He was expelled from the presence of God. (Ezekiel 28:16; John 8:24; Romans 1:25)

But the war was not a war over power and might. The war didn't center on territories or property. The weapons were not physical weapons that would someday be used by people on earth. To the contrary, the weapons of Satan were lies, flattery, deceit, innuendo, secrecy, manipulation, coercion, and intimidation - all used to misrepresent the truth about the Father and His Son, and to replace love with fear in the hearts of created beings. God fought back, but the weapons of God were not the weapons of the future world. God's weapons were truth, love, and freedom. The weapons of God were designed to demolish the stronghold of lies and deceit as well as the false arguments that misrepresent God, thus cleansing minds and restoring trust in God. (Zechariah 4:6; 2 Corinthians 10:3-5)

God and His angels presented the truth in love in order to combat the lies of Lucifer - now called the "dragon" - but the dragon and his angels presented more lies, continuing the fight against truth. However, their lies were not strong enough to persuade the entire universe to join their cause, so Lucifer and his followers found no place of sympathy in heaven. He was sent to a far corner of the universe where further evidence would be revealed and the war would be concluded. That old serpent, the devil, the accuser, the liar known as Satan, was sent to a little place called Earth. And the angels who believed him - one-third of all of God's heavenly family - went with him. (Revelation 12:4, 7-9)

Chapter Three - Earth

The earth at that time was a dark mass with deep water in a small corner of the Milky Way. It was formless and without light. What a perfect object lesson God had chosen! This undeveloped void in space demonstrated so clearly the inevitable result of rejecting God and His methods of love. God's Spirit came and hovered above the darkness. Then God the Son said, "Let there be light," and the darkness disappeared. The mass of matter forming the featureless core was used by the Son throughout creation week. That ancient matter, which God had previously made, He shaped into a sphere and caused to spin on its axis. This was the first day of the creation of earth and its solar system, where humans would be made in God's image to govern earth as God governs his universe. God doesn't win the war for hearts and minds with claims and proclamations. He provides evidence that reveals the truth. (Genesis 1:2-3; Job 38:4-7; John 8:32; 1 Corinthians 4:9)

On the second day the Son created an atmosphere with breathable air. He separated the waters, creating a protective layer above the atmosphere, while keeping water upon the earth with the atmosphere in between.
(Genesis 1:6, 7)

On the third day the Son brought forth dry ground and called it land. He gathered the waters together and called them seas.

Then the Son filled the earth with vegetation of all kinds: trees, flowers, fruits, and every beautiful and health-promoting plant.

All that the Son created was perfect, and there was no noxious or poisonous growth, no thorn or thistle, no toxic or harmful herb. (Genesis 1:9-12)

On day four Jesus created the sun, moon, and planets (stars) of Earth's solar system.

The sun would provide light during the day, and the moon during the night.

The rotational relationship between the earth, sun, and moon would be used to measure days, months, and years.

Everything He created was perfect. (Genesis 1:14-18)

...and the birds of the air.

He created every creature that lives in the water or flies above the land, endowing them with the ability to reproduce and fill the earth with life and beauty. (Genesis 1:20)

All the earth was created to operate on God's principle of other-centered giving—on the law of love. The plants were created to give oxygen to the animals, and the animals gave carbon dioxide back to the plants, both giving to the other - a perpetual circle of life.
It was the law of love in action.

The flowers produced pollen for the bees, and the bees pollinated the plants, each freely giving to the other—the basis of life. The electrons circled around the nucleus of the atom, the planets circled around the sun, the solar system circled in the Milky Way, and the galaxies spun their majestic paths throughout the universe. The circle of giving is the law of life, the foundation of God's throne. This planet—this earth—was created to magnify and reveal God's law of love. (Romans 1:20; 1 Corinthians 13:4; Ezekiel 10:1-10)

By day six, the intelligences throughout the ancient universe were overwhelmed with awe and bursting with anticipation. Their minds raced in wonder as they considered a lifeless, dark void transformed into a beautiful world, rich with life. This stunning evidence refuted Satan's allegations of equality with Jesus and the Father. The sons of God sang for joy and speculated about what the Son would create next. Then they watched in amazement as God gave the supreme evidence of their character of love—as the triune God formed humanity in their own image. (Job 38:4-8)

God the Father, Son, and Holy Spirit said, "Let us complete this lesson book, this microcosm of the universe, this theater designed to answer the allegations that Satan has brought against us.

Let us make humankind in our image - with the ability to think and reason - and in our likeness. Let's make them free to govern this planet, utilizing the methods we use in governing the universe.

Let's give them the ability to come into unity and create beings in their image, as we come into unity and create beings in ours. Let's let them rule over the creatures on this planet, as we rule over the universe, and let them reveal the truth about our character of love." (1 Corinthians 4:9; Genesis 1:26)

So God the Son created humankind in His own image: two separate beings, yet one in mind, purpose, substance, method, principle, motive, and authority.

Two beings operating on the principle of selfless love, constantly seeking the welfare and good of the other. As they shared themselves with each other in love - an act that would bring forth new life - they created an outflow for their love. In harmony with God's design, they were to give of themselves constantly for the protection, health, and happiness of their children. They were given authority to govern the planet, and all creation was in harmony with their rule of love. (Genesis 1:27-28)

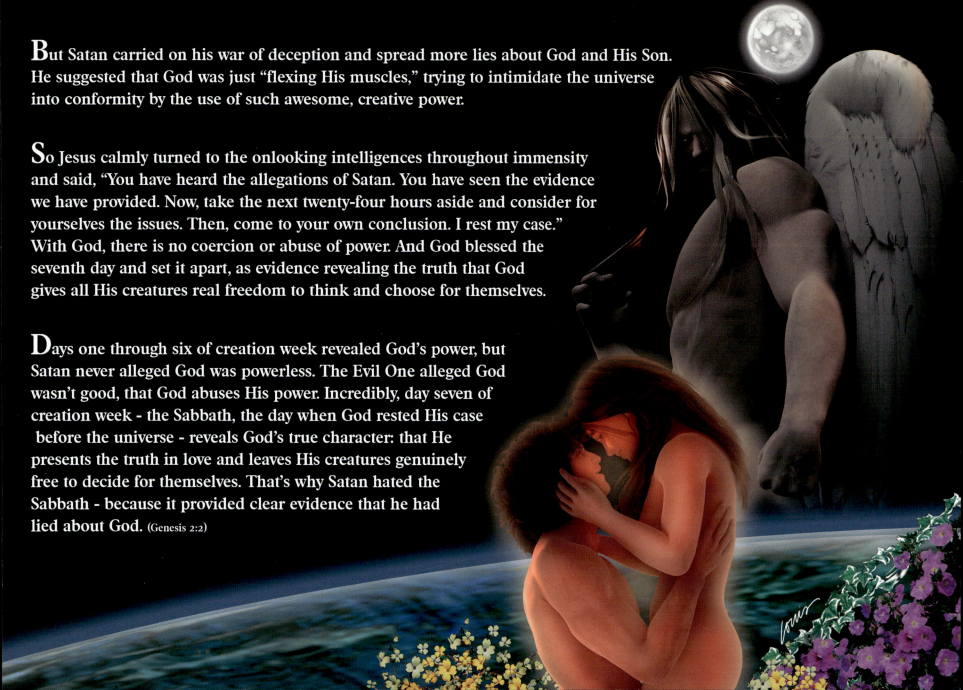

But Satan carried on his war of deception and spread more lies about God and His Son. He suggested that God was just "flexing His muscles," trying to intimidate the universe into conformity by the use of such awesome, creative power.

So Jesus calmly turned to the onlooking intelligences throughout immensity and said, "You have heard the allegations of Satan. You have seen the evidence we have provided. Now, take the next twenty-four hours aside and consider for yourselves the issues. Then, come to your own conclusion. I rest my case." With God, there is no coercion or abuse of power. And God blessed the seventh day and set it apart, as evidence revealing the truth that God gives all His creatures real freedom to think and choose for themselves.

Days one through six of creation week revealed God's power, but Satan never alleged God was powerless. The Evil One alleged God wasn't good, that God abuses His power. Incredibly, day seven of creation week - the Sabbath, the day when God rested His case before the universe - reveals God's true character: that He presents the truth in love and leaves His creatures genuinely free to decide for themselves. That's why Satan hated the Sabbath - because it provided clear evidence that he had lied about God. (Genesis 2:2)

God created a beautiful garden in Eden to be a home for Adam and Eve. He provided them with trees of all types, each offering food that was beautiful to behold and wonderful to eat. In the middle of the garden He planted a tree whose fruit bestowed perfect physical health - the Tree of Life.

God the Son gave them everything on the entire planet to possess, but reserved one tree - also in the middle of the garden - as an opportunity to exercise their power of choice and thus develop mature character. It was called the Tree of Knowledge of Good and Evil. (Genesis 2:9)

The Son put Adam and Eve in the Garden of Eden to tend and care for it. He told them, "Eat freely from every tree in the garden, but one tree is reserved - the Tree of Knowledge of Good and Evil. If you eat from it, you will most certainly die. If you value my methods of love, don't steal from the one tree that isn't your possession. If you do, you will corrupt yourself and separate yourself from me. You will violate the very principle upon which your life exists.

The result of that action is ruin and death." (Genesis 2:15-17)

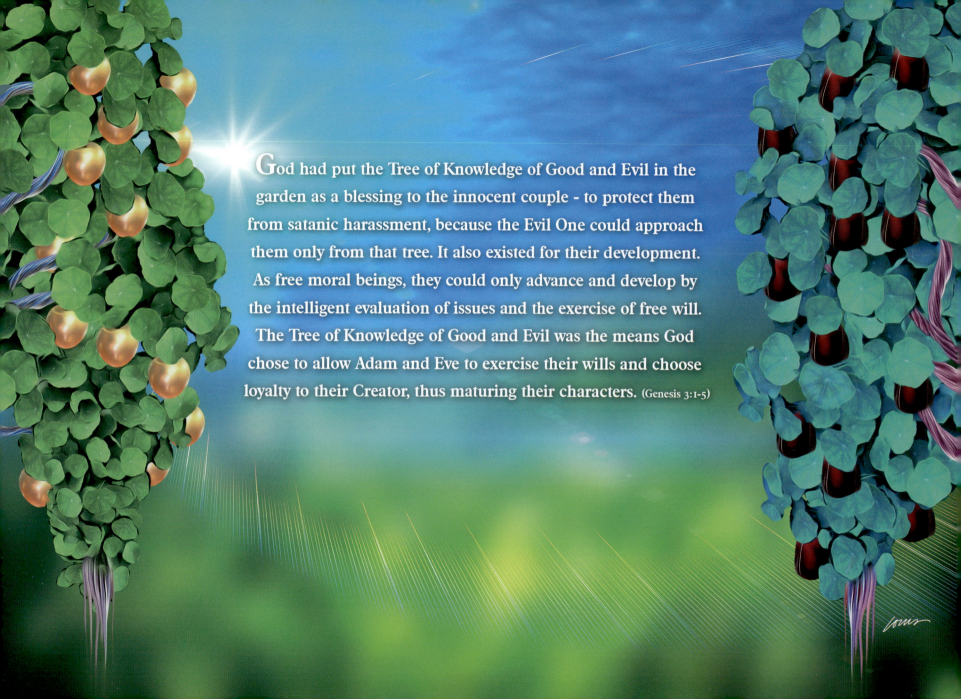

God had put the Tree of Knowledge of Good and Evil in the garden as a blessing to the innocent couple - to protect them from satanic harassment, because the Evil One could approach them only from that tree. It also existed for their development. As free moral beings, they could only advance and develop by the intelligent evaluation of issues and the exercise of free will. The Tree of Knowledge of Good and Evil was the means God chose to allow Adam and Eve to exercise their wills and choose loyalty to their Creator, thus maturing their characters. (Genesis 3:1-5)

Satan was desperate to undermine the lesson Adam and Eve were designed to reveal to the universe. So he used a serpent as a medium to confuse, seduce, and deceive Eve. He used the same strategy on her that he had used on the brilliant angels in heaven: he raised questions about God's trustworthiness.

He said, "Did God really tell you that if you eat of the tree in the middle of the garden you will die?

Oh no you won't. Look at me! I am only a mere serpent, yet because I ate of the tree I can now speak. God knows that when you - in your superior state - eat of the tree, you will become as powerful and all-knowing as God Himself. He's trying to keep this information from you.

You really can't trust what God says."

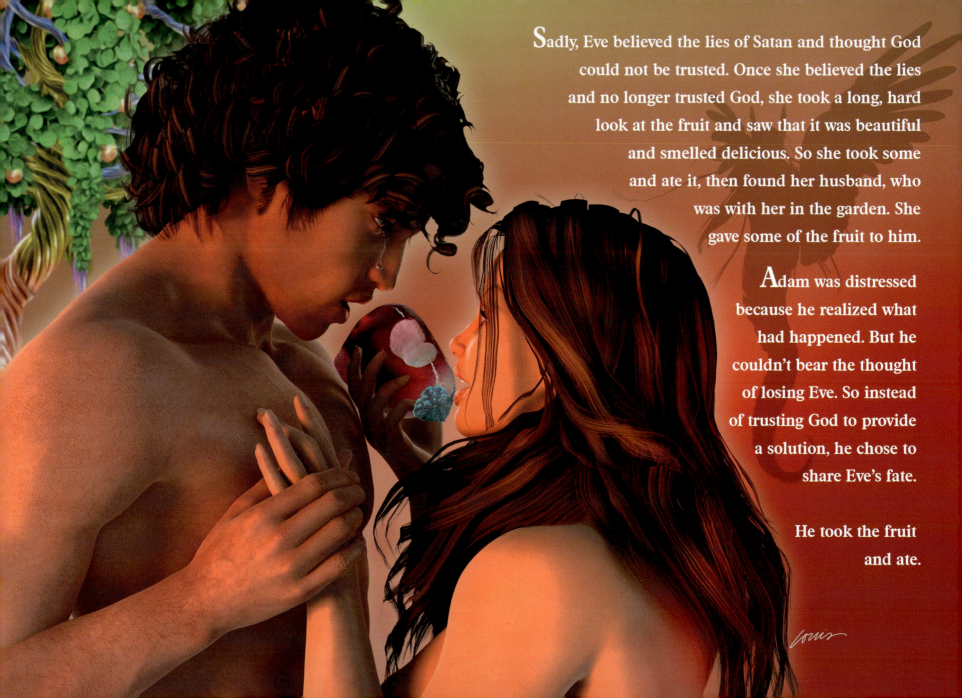

Immediately, they were changed. Their minds were infected with a destructive element. Their happy, peaceful state, their joy and contentment, their love and kindness, were displaced.

Love and trust were quickly supplanted by selfishness and fear. The principle of survival of the fittest infected the entire earth.

Without divine intervention, their condition was terminal.

(Genesis 3:6-7)

Then God said, "Adam, who told you that you were naked?

You didn't hear me condemn you.

Have you eaten from the only tree I told you to avoid? Adam, it's your own conscience condemning you, because your actions have changed you.

Believing lies about me has displaced love and peace with fear and selfishness.

Adam, I am not the one you need to fear. I am here to save you."
(Genesis 3:11)

Then Adam revealed how completely his character was twisted, how thoroughly his heart was infected with selfishness, how totally dominated he was by the principle of survival of the fittest.

Instead of lovingly offering to sacrifice himself to save Eve, instead of taking responsibility for his own conduct, he attempted to blame both Eve and God for his actions. He offered up Eve as a scapegoat, trying to exonerate himself. He said, "It was that woman you gave me, she brought me the fruit, and I ate it." (Genesis 3:12)

The angels in heaven were confused and longed to see the truth of what was happening. God's evidence, humanity, created in His image to reveal the truth about God, now revealed falsehoods about God. Adam's behavior suggested that, if God were like Adam, then God would sacrifice His creatures to protect Himself. Adam's behavior now supported Satan's lies about God. Adam was selfish, and God's law of love was no longer written in his heart. (1 Peter 1:12)

Yet all was not lost. God knew - though the cost would be great - that His creation could still be healed and restored. In love, He disclosed His plan to send a Savior - a divine hero - to do personal battle in order to finish the mission Adam failed to complete. Even more, He planned to restore all that had been lost through Adam's fall. Jesus would come to earth and in person overcome the enemy, defeat the infection of selfishness, write God's law of love again into the heart and restore His creation back into unity with His heart of love.

All was not lost. There was hope - hope in the Promised One to come. (Genesis 3:15)

Therefore, Jesus - God the Son - had committed Himself as the healing solution. Since Adam failed in his mission to reveal the truth about God, and since the earth was now infected with the principle of survival of the fittest, God implemented the plan that had been agreed upon long ago. The Father, the Son, and the Spirit began the process to heal and restore creation back to perfection. (1 Peter 1:19-20; John 17:4-6)

If humankind was to be healed, creation redeemed, and the universe secured, the power of sin and the destructiveness of Satan must be held in check in order to allow time for God's healing plan to be realized.

Therefore, God immediately began intercession: inserting Himself directly into the natural course of sin and into the midst of the destructive flow of Satan's power. God interceded in the heart and mind of man and woman, instilling a desire for good, a desire for healing. He wooed and called Adam and Eve, and uncovered Satan's hidden agendas. God also interceded on humankind's behalf with the very forces of evil, holding in check Satan's power to destroy. Eventually, through Christ, God would intercede with sin's destructive force by becoming incarnate - by becoming flesh - in order to eradicate sin and perfectly restore humanity back to God's design.

(Genesis 3:15; 2 Kings 6:17; Job 1:10; Zechariah 3:1-5; Romans 8:26, 31-34; 2 Corinthians 5:21; Revelation 7:1-3)

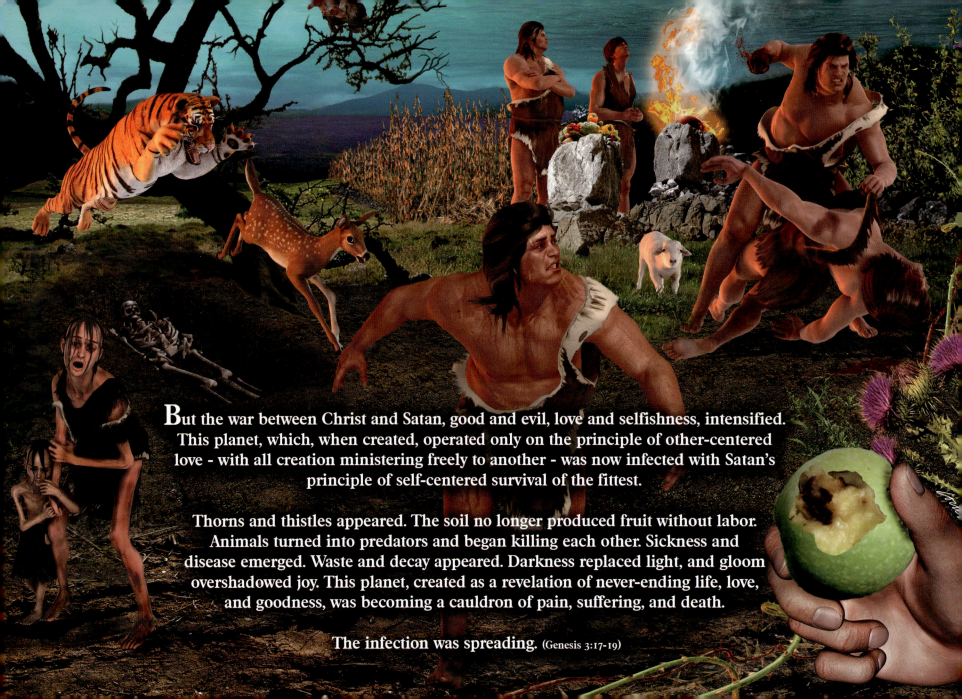

But the war between Christ and Satan, good and evil, love and selfishness, intensified. This planet, which, when created, operated only on the principle of other-centered love - with all creation ministering freely to another - was now infected with Satan's principle of self-centered survival of the fittest.

Thorns and thistles appeared. The soil no longer produced fruit without labor. Animals turned into predators and began killing each other. Sickness and disease emerged. Waste and decay appeared. Darkness replaced light, and gloom overshadowed joy. This planet, created as a revelation of never-ending life, love, and goodness, was becoming a cauldron of pain, suffering, and death.

The infection was spreading. (Genesis 3:17-19)

Chapter Seven - Earth's Early Skirmishes

Satan was alarmed when God announced His plan to save mankind.

The Evil One recognized his victory was not assured, his triumph not complete, his kingdom not secure. He realized he must work with all his power to oppose God's plan and, if possible, prevent the Promised One from ever coming to earth. So he inflamed men's fears and aroused their passions.

Cruelty, abuse, and violence increased. Minds were darkened, kindness disappeared, and men killed for the sport of it.
(Genesis 6:11-13)

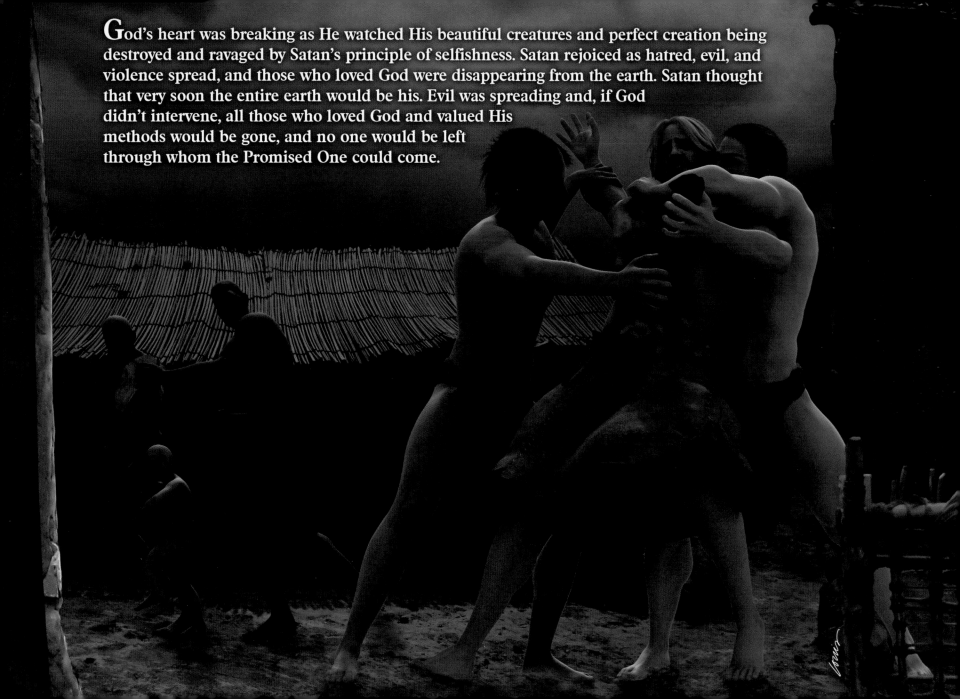

God's heart was breaking as He watched His beautiful creatures and perfect creation being destroyed and ravaged by Satan's principle of selfishness. Satan rejoiced as hatred, evil, and violence spread, and those who loved God were disappearing from the earth. Satan thought that very soon the entire earth would be his. Evil was spreading and, if God didn't intervene, all those who loved God and valued His methods would be gone, and no one would be left through whom the Promised One could come.

In the aftermath of the flood God provided the rainbow as a beautiful promise that water would never again destroy the entire earth. But Satan began undermining trust in God and working to close the avenue for the Messiah to come. Humanity soon preferred Satan's version of God and opposed the Creator. They said, "Let's build a tower that will take us into heaven and we can save ourselves." So God, in order to slow the spread of deception, confused their languages. By doing so, each separate group would have to be communicated to individually, thus the infection of lies would be slowed and the channel would remain open for the Savior to come. (Gen 11:1-9)

The representative heads of all creation were gathering together in heaven, and Satan thought, If I can twist God's actions and misrepresent His motives, then maybe I can win more sinless beings to my cause. Satan reasoned that if he were subtle enough, maybe some of God's loyal sons would fail to realize that God put many of His earthly children to rest in order to keep an avenue open to heal and redeem. Maybe he could deceive them into believing God was abusive and coercive and can't be trusted. And maybe he could simultaneously corner God into giving him access to destroy those few remaining loyal to Him on earth. So Satan went to this meeting in heaven, claiming to be the rightful representative of the earth. (Job 1:6, 7)

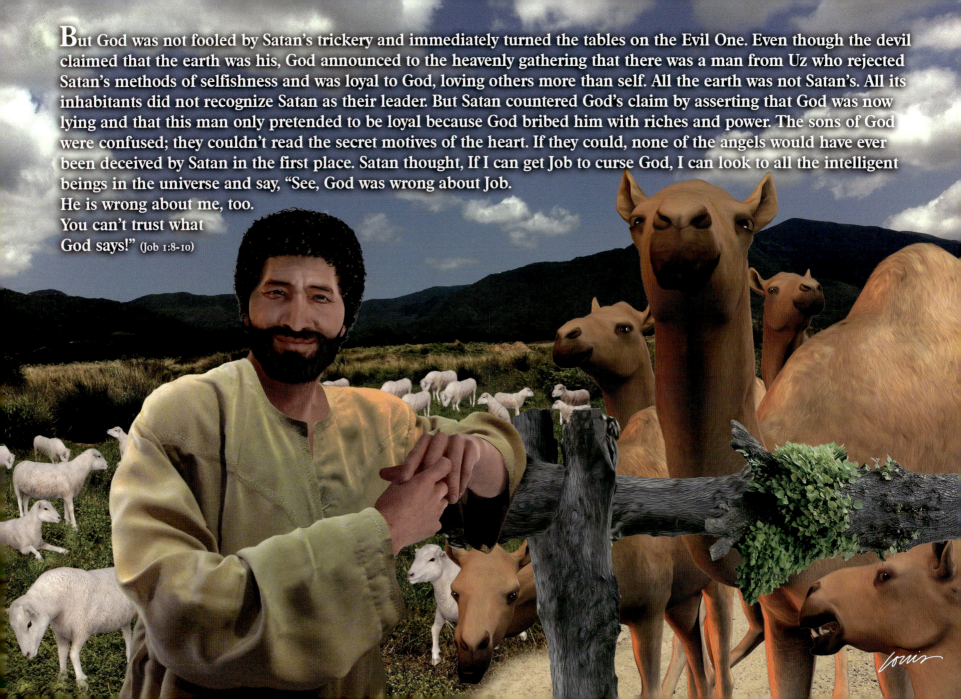

But God was not fooled by Satan's trickery and immediately turned the tables on the Evil One. Even though the devil claimed that the earth was his, God announced to the heavenly gathering that there was a man from Uz who rejected Satan's methods of selfishness and was loyal to God, loving others more than self. All the earth was not Satan's. All its inhabitants did not recognize Satan as their leader. But Satan countered God's claim by asserting that God was now lying and that this man only pretended to be loyal because God bribed him with riches and power. The sons of God were confused; they couldn't read the secret motives of the heart. If they could, none of the angels would have ever been deceived by Satan in the first place. Satan thought, If I can get Job to curse God, I can look to all the intelligent beings in the universe and say, "See, God was wrong about Job.

He is wrong about me, too.

You can't trust what God says!" (Job 1:8-10)

Again, wickedness, selfishness, cruelty, inhospitality, and violence began to spread. Cities on a fertile plain became a vile source of total depravity and self-centeredness - attributes that threatened to spread throughout the earth and destroy any channel through which the Promised One could come. So, once again, God, with breaking heart, intervened and put those cities to rest in order to keep open the avenue for His ultimate cure.

(Genesis 18–19; Ezekiel 16:49-50)

Chapter Eight – A Family From Ur

There was another man, this time from Ur, whose mind was open to God and who longed to be healed of the infection of selfishness. This man, Abraham, was willing to follow God's treatment plan and cooperate with Him for healing and restoration. He talked with God and was considered a true friend. God chose this man - and his descendants - as the avenue through which the Promised One would come, the channel through which God's remedy for the entire world would be realized. God chose this man's family as His helpers to act out and teach the story of the war between good and evil, and His plan to save, heal, and restore His creation. (Genesis 12:1-3)

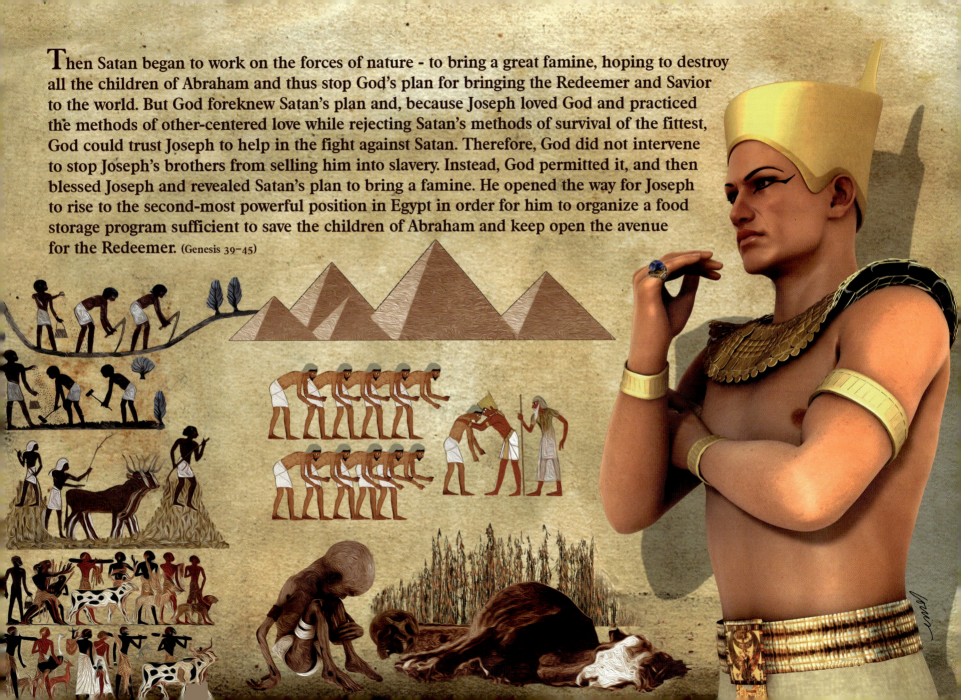

Satan continued his attacks against God and His plan to bring a Redeemer and cure. Once again, he attempted to destroy the channel through which God's remedy would come. A new pharaoh arose in Egypt, one who did not know Joseph, and Satan inflamed his fears and selfishness until he ordered that the children of Abraham, the Hebrews, be enslaved.

But God did not abandon those He had chosen to teach the truths about the universal war and be the conduit for the Savior. Instead He used their circumstances as an object lesson to teach the truth about the war and His plan to heal and restore. God intervened and sent them a redeemer, Moses, to stand against the power that enslaved them, and to bring liberty and freedom and to lead them to the earthly Promised Land. God permitted these events to reveal, in miniature, His plan to redeem the race from the enslavement of selfishness and sin.

(Exodus 6:1-12)

But Satan had confused the minds of the people, both Hebrew and Egyptian, with a multitude of false gods. But God loved all the people and had Moses reveal, through ten therapeutic interventions, that the gods of the Egyptians were not real. Hebrew or Egyptian, who trusted God, death would not touch. Satan was furious as he saw truth demolish his deep-rooted lies. (Exodus chapters 7-12)

Just as Moses defeated pharaoh, Jesus would someday defeat Satan. Just as Moses brought freedom from Egyptian bondage, Christ would bring freedom from the bondage of sin. Just as Moses led them to an earthly "Promised Land," Christ would lead humankind to the heavenly land of promise. And just as the people rebelled and murmured against Moses, so too would many murmur and rebel against Christ.

(Exodus 2:10-15; 3:1–12:42)

Because the infection of selfishness so permeated their hearts and minds, and because love was almost totally obscured, God, in love, gave them regulations and rules to help them regain order and to protect them from selfish exploitation and abuse. These rules would remain in place until the day the true remedy would come and selfishness would be eradicated forever. (Exodus 21:1–23:9; Leviticus 18:1–20:27)

God didn't leave them with the terminal diagnosis of selfishness. He also promised that a Redeemer with the cure for their condition would arrive.

However, because their minds were so darkened and their understanding so primitive, God had to stoop down and teach them like children. He designed a little theater complete with costumes, props, and roles to play in order to teach His plan. After all, what does one do with a group of people who saw the ten plagues of Egypt, who walked through the Red Sea on dry ground, who witnessed the pillar of fire by night and the cloud by day, who heard the thundering of God at Sinai, and who were fed manna in the desert – and then forty short days later forgot God and organized an orgy around a calf made from their own jewelry by their own hands?

What does one do?

One takes them to the sandbox and gives them roles to play in reenacting the great unfolding drama of salvation. God gave them the sanctuary service with all its rights and rituals to teach them the truths of the great drama and His amazing plan to heal. (Exodus 7:1-18:27; 23:14-31:11; 32:1-29; 36:1-40:33; Leviticus 1:1-9:24; 16:1-34)

But before Jesus could implement the little theater to teach his healing plan, a crisis broke out in heaven. Satan stirred up more doubts amongst the celestial beings. He alleged that God's ways don't work. He pointed the angels toward the events just transpired in Egypt and said, "Look at those people! They are beyond healing. Even after signs, wonders, and miraculous delivery from Egypt, they prefer a golden calf. They don't want God and they can't be restored to God's ways. God is misleading you."

And we watchers, along with the cherubim and seraphim, were riveted. We watched as Jesus, sounding angry with the people, went to Moses. He made it appear He was going to wipe out the Hebrews and He even offered to make a great nation from Moses' descendants. And what did Moses do? Amazingly, rather than accepting exaltation for himself, Moses revealed that selfishness had been replaced with God's selfless love. He immediately argued for God's reputation and offered his life to save the people. Jesus turned to the angels and smiled, "Trust me, my methods work. Every human who trusts in me will be fully restored back to my design of love." (Exodus 32:1-14, 32; 1Corinthians 10:4)

God's teaching tools were so beautiful and simple. In the sanctuary service, the blood symbolized the life of the animal. The lamb symbolized the coming Savior. The sanctuary symbolized the temple where God dwells by His Spirit. That temple also represented the hearts and minds of His children.

Thus the blood of the lamb symbolized the life of the coming Messiah. The Messiah's life was illustrated throughout the sanctuary system to teach God's plan to restore His character in the hearts and minds of His children, thereby bringing life, health, rebirth, renewal, and recreation to His sin-infected children—purging the disease of selfishness and restoring His law of love in their hearts.
(Leviticus 17:11, 14; John 1:29, 36; 6:53-56; 1 Corinthians 3:16-17; 6:19; Hebrews 8:10)

God knew it would be many generations before the time would be right for the Redeemer to come and purge the infection of selfishness. So He provided guidance in the areas of health care, sanitation, and diet - all lovingly designed to protect from temporal sickness, pain, and suffering while promoting health for body and brain.

(Leviticus 11:1-15:32)

Satan recognized the danger if the lessons of the sanctuary service should be understood, so he immediately set about introducing distortions into the minds of God's helpers on the earth. He seduced them with heathen practices and further twisted their concept of God. He enticed them into paganism and the worship of angry and wrathful deities who required sacrifices and appeasement. They even offered their own children to these pagan gods and brought prostitutes into God's house. Satan led them to believe God was like their pagan deities, one who demanded payment, who took satisfaction in the suffering of the wicked, who was unforgiving and severe, and preferred bloody sacrifices in order to assuage His wrath. (Judges 3:7; 1 Kings 12:31-32; 14:22-24; 15:25-26, 33-34; 16:25-26, 30-31; 2 Kings 21:1-6)

But God was not like their pagan gods. He eventually came to hate His chosen people's sacrifices, their rituals, their feast days, their fasting, and their sabbaths, because they did these activities without engaging their minds and learned nothing from them. God had given them these ordinances as a means to motivate His people to think and thereby grow in understanding of His plan. Instead, the people stopped thinking and carried out the rituals as if there were redeeming value in the ritual itself. Even worse, they characterized God as if He were just like pagan gods—needing to be appeased. They completely lost sight of the reality that God simply wanted to heal them from selfishness and restore His law of love in their hearts. He wanted them to be kind, honest, gentle, and loving. He wanted their happiness and their good. (Psalm 51:17; Isaiah 1:10-18; 29:13; 58:4-8; Hosea 6:6; Amos 5:21-24; Micah 6:6-8; Hebrews 8:10)

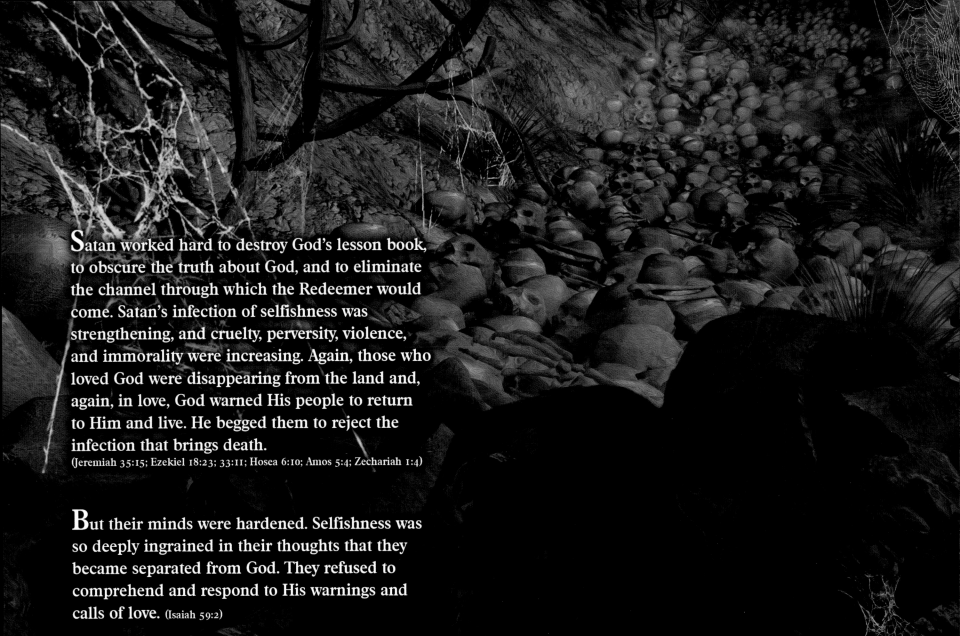

Satan worked hard to destroy God's lesson book, to obscure the truth about God, and to eliminate the channel through which the Redeemer would come. Satan's infection of selfishness was strengthening, and cruelty, perversity, violence, and immorality were increasing. Again, those who loved God were disappearing from the land and, again, in love, God warned His people to return to Him and live. He begged them to reject the infection that brings death.
(Jeremiah 35:15; Ezekiel 18:23; 33:11; Hosea 6:10; Amos 5:4; Zechariah 1:4)

But their minds were hardened. Selfishness was so deeply ingrained in their thoughts that they became separated from God. They refused to comprehend and respond to His warnings and calls of love. (Isaiah 59:2)

Chapter Eleven - Captivity

God's heart was breaking. He longed to heal His children, to protect them, restore them, and nurture them back to health. But they would not allow it. They rejected God and His methods of love and preferred Satan and his self-indulgent, "me first" ways. Satan exulted. He thought he would win. He thought he would destroy the avenue through which the Redeemer would come, preventing His arrival. In sadness beyond comprehension, God cried out, "How can I give you up? How can I let you go? But you are tied to your wickedness and bent on leaving me." (Hosea 4:17; 11:8)

So, in great sorrow, as the only means of preserving a remnant through which the Redeemer would come, God withdrew His protection and allowed the Chaldeans to come and take the children of Israel into captivity. Again Satan rejoiced, for he had led God's helpers to reject and misrepresent God while further obscuring the truth about His character of love. Satan redoubled his efforts to prevent the truth God was trying to teach from ever being understood by anyone, anywhere. (Ezekiel 12:13; 23:14-23)

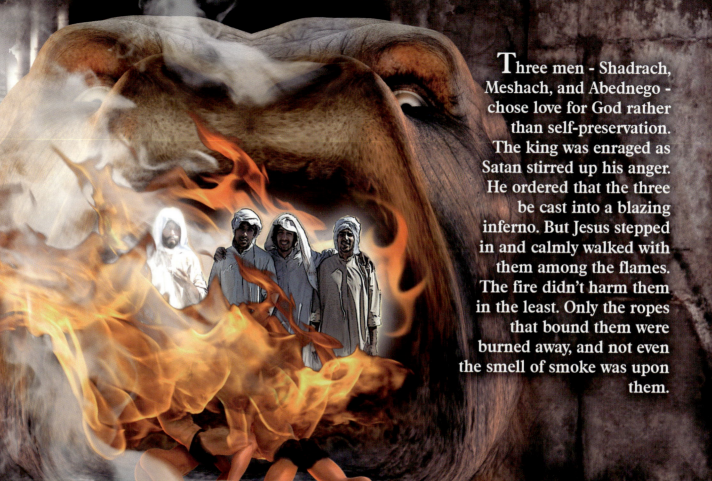

However, with His people in captivity, God did not abandon His faithful few. He blessed them with wisdom and talent beyond any peer. In the meantime, Satan inflamed the hatred, jealousy, and fear of the Chaldeans. He sought to coerce God's faithful few into betraying Him or be destroyed. Satan inspired the king to demand worship or be burned alive. The temptation to turn from God and save self was great, but love for God was even greater.

Three men - Shadrach, Meshach, and Abednego - chose love for God rather than self-preservation. The king was enraged as Satan stirred up his anger. He ordered that the three be cast into a blazing inferno. But Jesus stepped in and calmly walked with them among the flames. The fire didn't harm them in the least. Only the ropes that bound them were burned away, and not even the smell of smoke was upon them.

Satan's attempt to misrepresent God and destroy love for Him was foiled again.
(Daniel 1:19-20; 3:1-30)

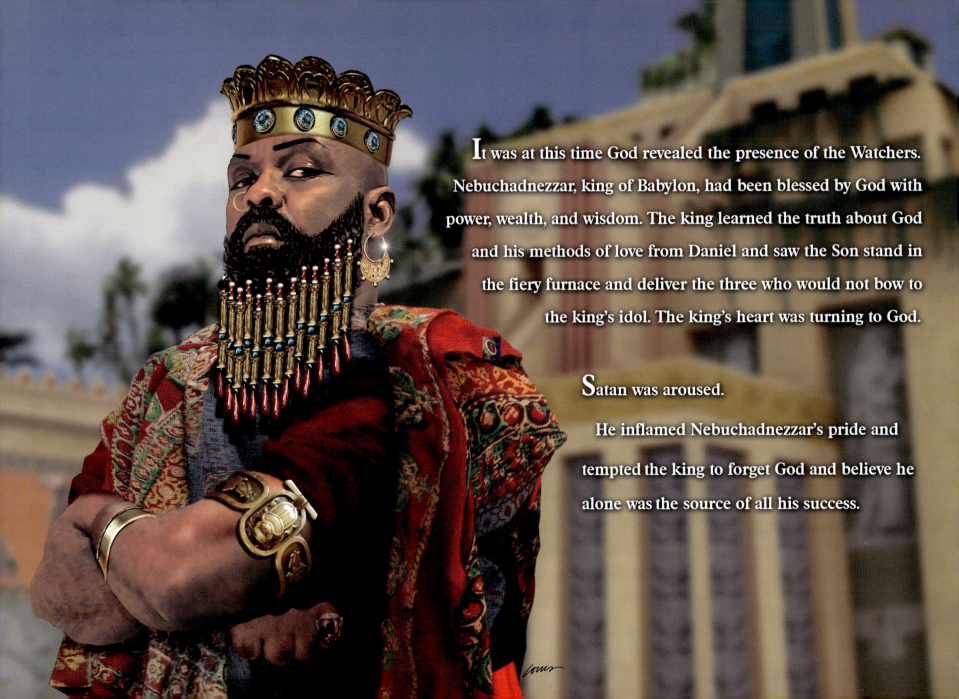

It was at this time God revealed the presence of the Watchers. Nebuchadnezzar, king of Babylon, had been blessed by God with power, wealth, and wisdom. The king learned the truth about God and his methods of love from Daniel and saw the Son stand in the fiery furnace and deliver the three who would not bow to the king's idol. The king's heart was turning to God.

Satan was aroused.

He inflamed Nebuchadnezzar's pride and tempted the king to forget God and believe he alone was the source of all his success.

So the Watchers assigned to Persia went to God with a plan to save the king. The Watchers recommended the king lose his sanity for seven years then be restored fully in mind and power, so that Nebuchadnezzar would realize all he had was a blessing from God. God smiled at the love he saw in the motivation of the Watchers and nodded, knowing their plan would work. So God sent the king a dream revealing to him what the Watchers had determined. One year later, the decree of the Watchers was fulfilled. (Daniel 4:13-23)

Satan was furious that his plot to destroy those who rejected selfishness and valued God's methods of selfless love had failed. He became more desperate to destroy those who revealed God's true character and eradicate any channel through which God could work. So, with a new earthly government in power, he again incited jealousy, evil-surmising, conniving, and selfish ambition. Soon another trap was laid for God's friends. The command was given: "Worship only the king or be thrown to the lions!" Daniel - like Shadrach, Meshach, and Abednego - chose love for God rather than seeking to save self.

As before, God chose to intervene and miraculously prevent the lions from devouring him. God's friend was safe, and Satan was defeated.

(Daniel 6:1-28)

Then Daniel talked with God and asked how long it would be until deliverance would come. How long would it be until God healed and restored His image in humanity? In response, God revealed to Daniel the very year in which the Promised One would come and restore righteousness, destroy evil, and provide the remedy that brings life. Four hundred and eighty-three years would pass from the decree to rebuild Jerusalem until the public appearance of the Messiah. Then three-and-a-half years would pass until the Messiah would complete His mission to defeat the enemy, free the captives, destroy the infection of selfishness, and reestablish love in the heart of humankind. (Daniel 9:20-26)

It was 457 BC when Artaxerxes the Great—the ruler of the Persian Empire—gave the decree to restore and rebuild Jerusalem. Israel was freed and returned to their homeland. The people reconstructed their stage—their mini-theater—and began, once again, to perform their roles in acting out the drama of the great war between good and evil. The time had been set. The clock had started. It would be 483 years from this decree until the Messiah would be anointed! (Ezra 7:8-26)

Did Satan sit idly by waiting for God's plan to be revealed? Oh, no! He again attacked God's helpers, using the influences of their pagan wives to tempt the children of Israel back into idolatry, cult worship, and fertility rights. But seventy years of captivity had taught them a painful lesson. Ezra stood up and opposed all reminders of foreign gods. So strong was his message and the desire to never again return to paganism that the Israelites sent away their heathen wives. They closed the avenue for perversity, degradation, and sensual indulgence. (Ezra 10:9-17)

So Satan crafted an even subtler deception. He led them to believe they had a special right to salvation, that God loved them more than others, that genetics, not character, is what determines fitness for heaven. He led them to believe God was an exacting taskmaster and that salvation was found in rituals performed in order to appease Him. Satan worked with all the perversity of his wicked mind to so misconstrue the truth about God that when He came and walked among them, they would hate and murder Him. (Jeremiah 31:35-37; Luke 18:9-12; John 4:9; Acts 7:51)

God the Father foreknew what was going to happen to His Son and revealed this to His friends the prophets. He saw Satan's continued attempts to destroy the avenue through which the Divine Hero would come to bring His remedy and cure. He also saw that, in order to reveal the truth and to cure humankind's terminal condition, His Son would have to suffer greatly. Not because God demanded it, but because the situation demanded it. There was no other way to win the war. God also knew that while He would not lay a hand on His Son or harm Him in any way, the price He would have to pay would be terribly high. His suffering would be beyond description. God also realized that men would misunderstand and blame Him for the suffering of Christ. They would say, "We esteemed Him stricken by God."

Satan exulted at the thought that he could so successfully distort the truth about God in the minds of men that even with God's Son standing in the flesh among them, telling them plainly, "If you've seen me you've seen the Father," most would believe his lies about God and see Him as a cruel tyrant who demanded a blood payment in order to be just. God knew that the only hope for man was in sending His Son - one equal with Himself - to roll back the moral darkness, reveal the truth, expose the liar, exonerate God, and bring the remedy that would heal His creation. But God knew that, in spite of His best efforts, many would prefer the lie and reject His Son. (Psalm 22; Isaiah 53:4-5; Daniel 9:25-27; Amos 3:7)

So, because Adam failed in the purpose of His creation - to reveal the truth about God - and because the world was now infected with selfishness that, if unchecked, would lead only to death, Jesus became a real human being. Unlike Lucifer, Jesus didn't think His equality with God was something to be grasped, and He became a lowly servant. He established His temple - the temple of His body - among the earth's inhabitants in order to defeat Satan and bring God's remedy to the world. Through this act, all would see the glory of His character - the character of the one and only true God who came from and reveals the Father, the source of all grace and truth. (John 1:14; Philippians 2:6-7)

When the time was right, God intervened and sent His Son. Jesus was born of a sin - infected human mother; born a real human baby with a weakened humanity that had been damaged by the law of sin and death. He did this in order to purify and cleanse humanity and purge all people from the infection of selfishness that brings death.
(Daniel 9:20-26; Matthew 1:18-24; John 1:1-3, 14; Galatians 4:4,5; Hebrews 2:14, 4:15)

He was able to purify humanity of sin because, even though His mother was infected with selfishness and sin His Father was God. Christ was born with His heart and mind in full unity and oneness with His Father. In Jesus was found original life - not borrowed, not derived, the pure life of God that purges the infection of sin and selfishness and enlightens the mind about God, His character, methods, and principles. This life reconnected humankind with God and His methods of love.
(Isaiah 7:14; 9:6; Matthew 1:20; John 1:4; Hebrews 5:8)

Satan recognized that his illicit hold on the earth was not secure - that one mighty in love could overthrow his hold on humankind. So he inspired his servant Herod to kill baby Jesus long before He could complete His mission, before Jesus could reveal the truth and procure the remedy.

While many of the professed followers of God had believed Satan's lies and thought a mere blood payment from a perfect sacrifice was necessary for salvation, Satan knew that killing the sinless baby Jesus would stop God's plan cold and prevent Him from saving the world.

Thus God protected the baby Jesus and made provision for His safety so that He could fulfill His mission to reveal the truth about God, expose Satan as the liar and fraud he was, reveal the destructiveness of sin, and restore God's love into God's spiritual temple - the heart and mind of humankind. He would do this by His own victorious life and self-sacrificing death.

(Matthew 2:13-16; John 10:17-18; Hebrews 8:10)

He grew and developed physically, mentally, emotionally, and spiritually just as all human beings do through trials, education, experience, and communion with His Father. But, unlike all other human beings, Jesus grew in perfect love, developing in His humanity a perfect Godlike character. He accomplished this through constant, complete, and total victory over the temptations of selfishness. He became the Remedy—the source of healing for all humanity. (Luke 2:4-16, 39-40, 51; Hebrews 5:7-8)

The world was in darkness: darkness about God, His character, methods, and principles. The light of Jesus' life shone into those minds darkened by Satan's lies. But man's darkened mind did not understand it.
(Isaiah 60:2; John 1:5)

Chapter Thirteen – Ministry

When Jesus was fully grown, and His physical, mental, and spiritual powers had matured, He entered His public ministry. In a.d. 27, exactly 483 years after the decree to restore and rebuild Jerusalem had been handed down, Christ was baptized, was anointed by the Holy Spirit and went out to the desert to confront, overcome, and vanquish Satan, confronting face-to-face his methods of generating selfishness in God's children.

But He resisted by choosing to humble Himself in loving obedience to God. Then, Satan tempted Christ to save Himself by worshiping Satan. But He fought back by choosing love for God over any attempt at self-preservation. There in the desert, in the person of Jesus Christ - sheathed in the humanity He took upon Himself - love conquered selfishness! Satan was furious.

(Daniel 9:20-26; Ezra 7:8-26; Matthew 3:13–4:11; John 1:32-34)

After defeating Satan in the desert, Christ went forward to reveal the truth about God and promote His methods of love that would set free those held in the bondage of sin and selfishness. His mission was to enlighten hearts and minds to the true remedy and, in doing so, heal His creation. (Isaiah 61:1; Matthew 4:17; Luke 4:17-19)

As the Jewish Passover was approaching, Jesus traveled to Jerusalem to begin His public ministry. He went to the Temple - that great, towering object lesson designed to teach God's self-sacrificing plan for bringing all things in heaven and on earth back into unity with Him.

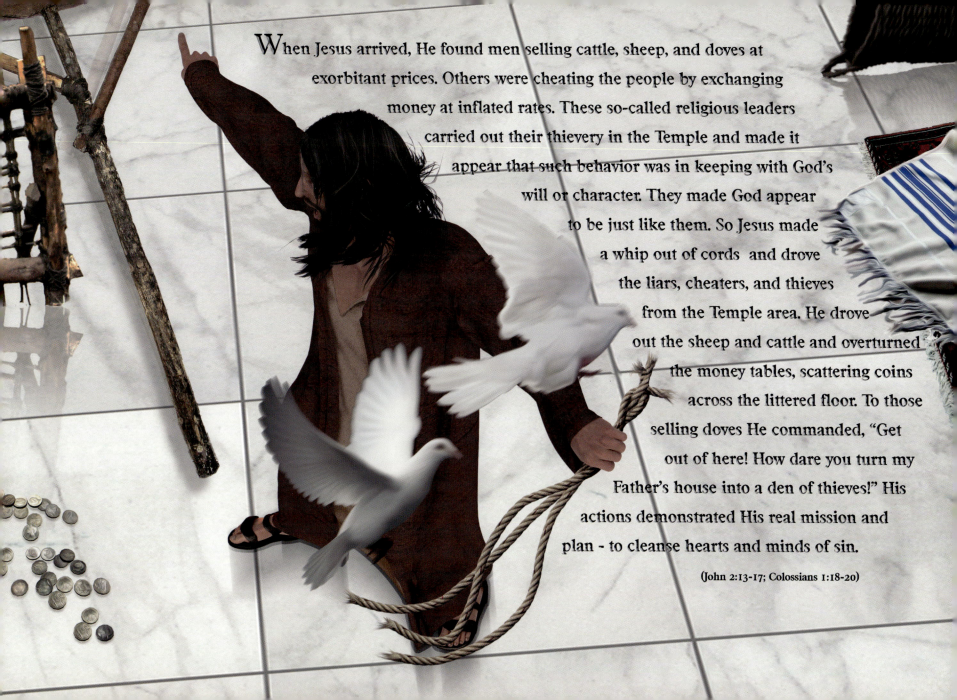

When Jesus arrived, He found men selling cattle, sheep, and doves at exorbitant prices. Others were cheating the people by exchanging money at inflated rates. These so-called religious leaders carried out their thievery in the Temple and made it appear that such behavior was in keeping with God's will or character. They made God appear to be just like them. So Jesus made a whip out of cords and drove the liars, cheaters, and thieves from the Temple area. He drove out the sheep and cattle and overturned the money tables, scattering coins across the littered floor. To those selling doves He commanded, "Get out of here! How dare you turn my Father's house into a den of thieves!" His actions demonstrated His real mission and plan - to cleanse hearts and minds of sin.

(John 2:13-17; Colossians 1:18-20)

The Jewish leaders eventually came back and demanded: "What miracle can you perform to prove to us that you have the right and authority to come in here and change what we have been doing for hundreds of years?"

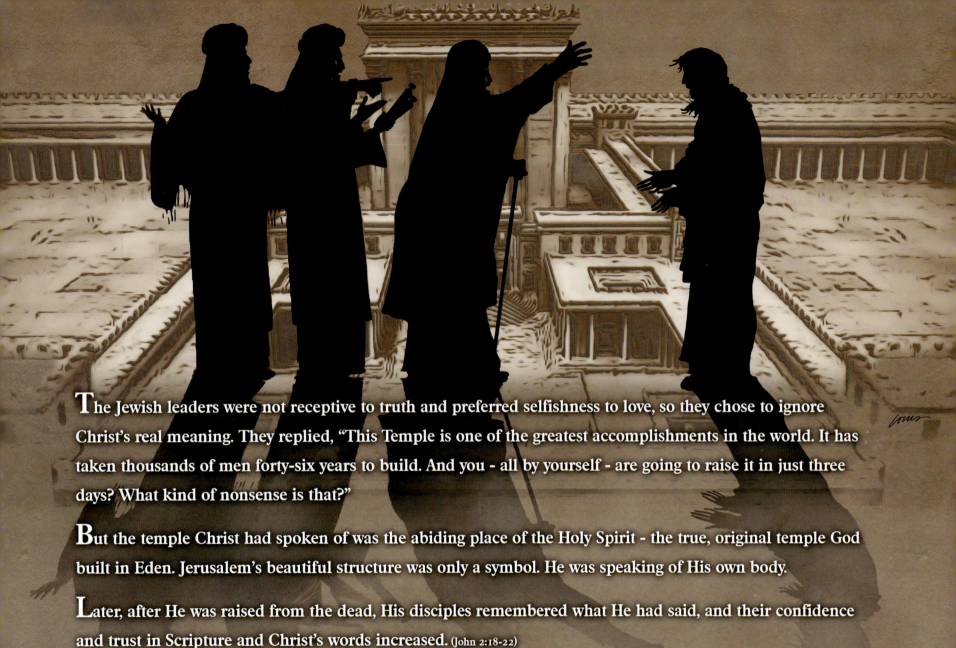

The Jewish leaders were not receptive to truth and preferred selfishness to love, so they chose to ignore Christ's real meaning. They replied, "This Temple is one of the greatest accomplishments in the world. It has taken thousands of men forty-six years to build. And you - all by yourself - are going to raise it in just three days? What kind of nonsense is that?"

But the temple Christ had spoken of was the abiding place of the Holy Spirit - the true, original temple God built in Eden. Jerusalem's beautiful structure was only a symbol. He was speaking of His own body.

Later, after He was raised from the dead, His disciples remembered what He had said, and their confidence and trust in Scripture and Christ's words increased. (John 2:18-22)

Chapter Fourteen ~ Teaching

After the confrontation at the Temple, one of the leading religious leaders in Israel - a man named Nicodemus - came to see Jesus. He snuck in at night because he didn't want to be associated publicly with this "troublemaker." Jesus made it plain to Nicodemus that no one could go to heaven unless he or she was recreated from within, possessed a new heart, was reborn, and had selfishness removed and God's law of love restored in his or her heart and mind. He explained that humankind was in a terminal condition and those who rejected the remedy He came to offer could never heal themselves and were destined to die. But all who accepted Him would be healed and live eternally.

Nicodemus was confused, so Christ spelled it out plainly.

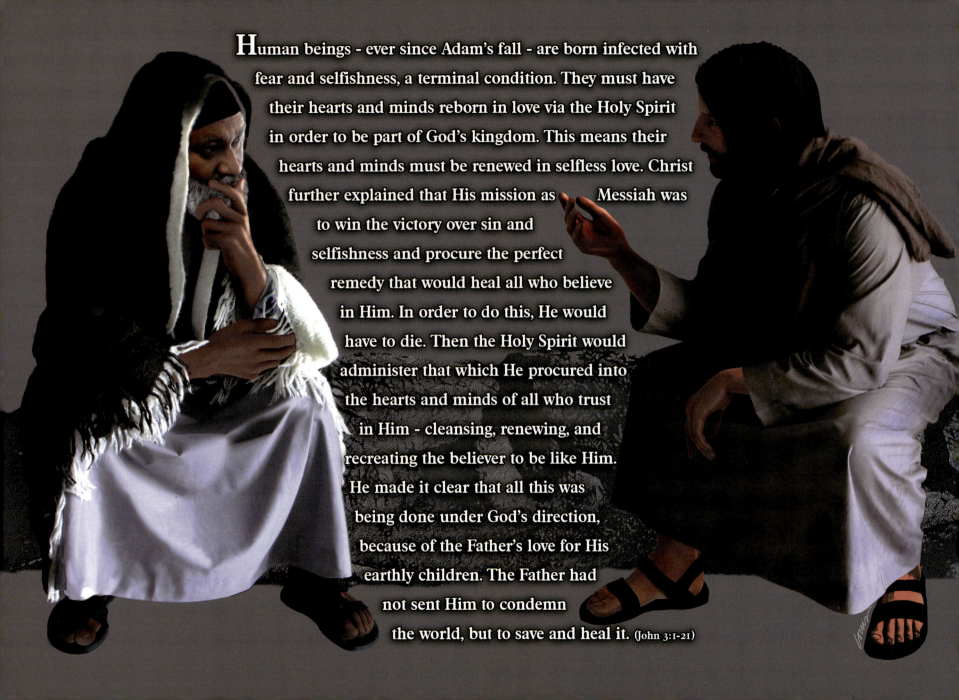

Jesus' life was a continual demonstration of the truth about God, His character, and His methods. He was working to dispel the lies of Satan and reveal to the world that God the Father is just like Him in every way.
(John 14:8-9)

Jesus told her that He possessed the secret water of eternal life - the water of God's love that when internalized, transforms the heart and overflows to others. The woman eagerly requested this water. But Jesus knew that if she drank of it - if she really internalized His love in her heart - major changes in her life would result. So, in order to help her realize this and be prepared, He told her to go get her husband.

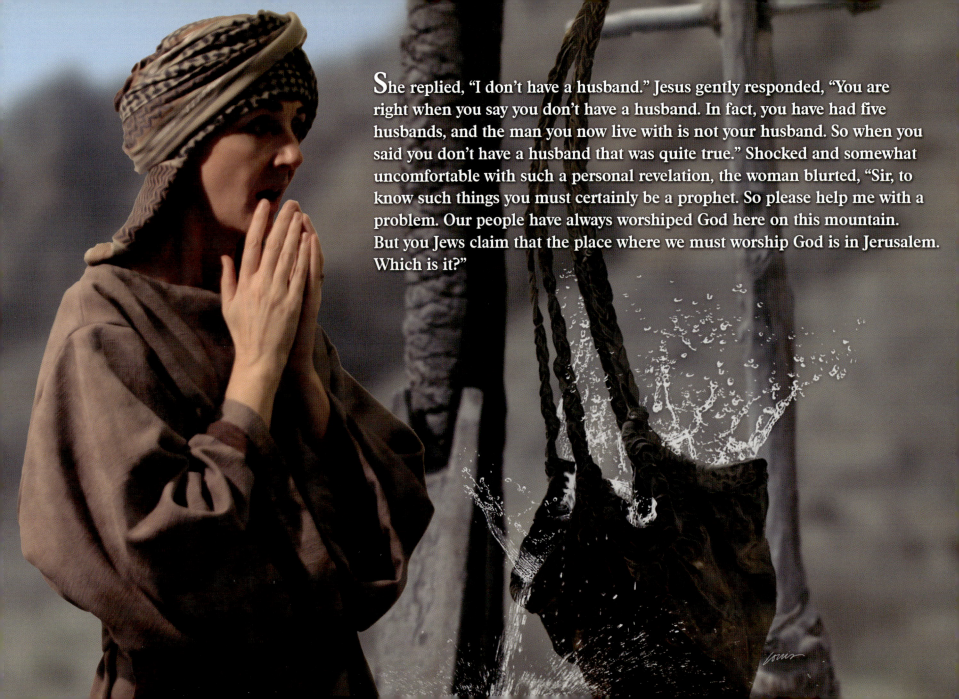

She replied, "I don't have a husband." Jesus gently responded, "You are right when you say you don't have a husband. In fact, you have had five husbands, and the man you now live with is not your husband. So when you said you don't have a husband that was quite true." Shocked and somewhat uncomfortable with such a personal revelation, the woman blurted, "Sir, to know such things you must certainly be a prophet. So please help me with a problem. Our people have always worshiped God here on this mountain. But you Jews claim that the place where we must worship God is in Jerusalem. Which is it?"

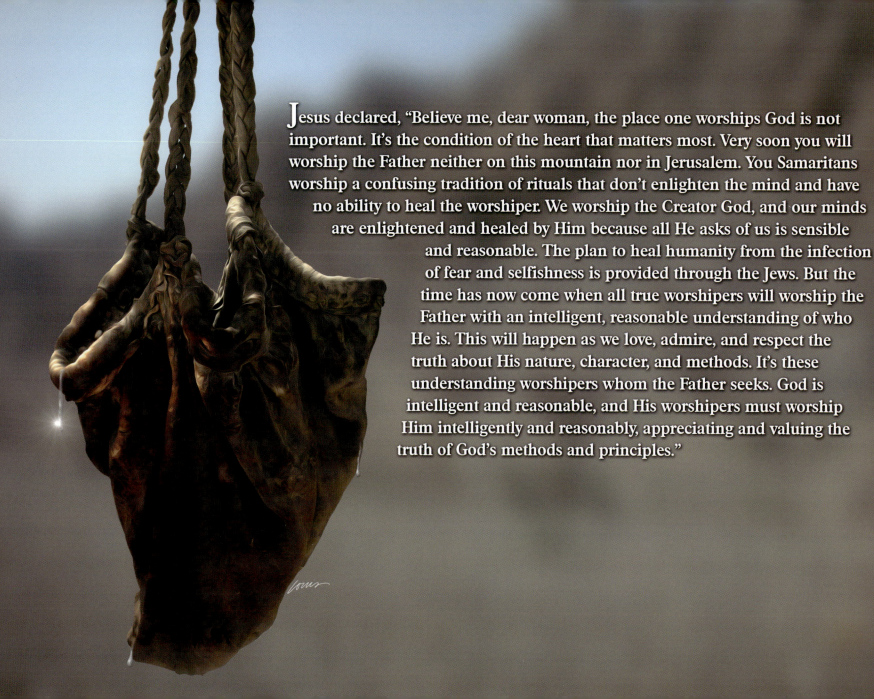

Jesus declared, "Believe me, dear woman, the place one worships God is not important. It's the condition of the heart that matters most. Very soon you will worship the Father neither on this mountain nor in Jerusalem. You Samaritans worship a confusing tradition of rituals that don't enlighten the mind and have no ability to heal the worshiper. We worship the Creator God, and our minds are enlightened and healed by Him because all He asks of us is sensible and reasonable. The plan to heal humanity from the infection of fear and selfishness is provided through the Jews. But the time has now come when all true worshipers will worship the Father with an intelligent, reasonable understanding of who He is. This will happen as we love, admire, and respect the truth about His nature, character, and methods. It's these understanding worshipers whom the Father seeks. God is intelligent and reasonable, and His worshipers must worship Him intelligently and reasonably, appreciating and valuing the truth of God's methods and principles."

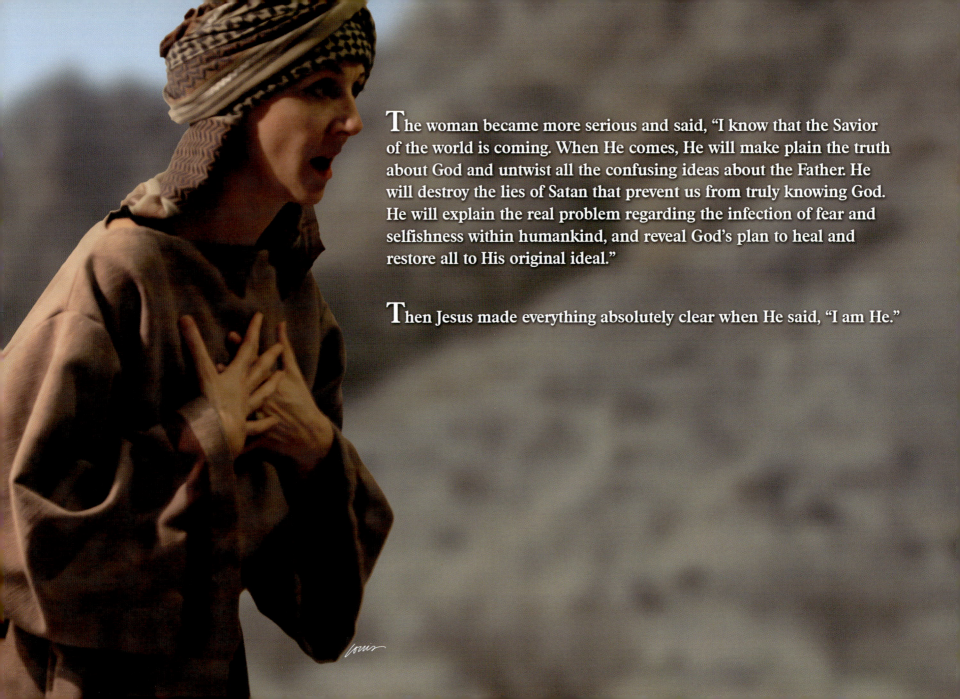

The woman became more serious and said, "I know that the Savior of the world is coming. When He comes, He will make plain the truth about God and untwist all the confusing ideas about the Father. He will destroy the lies of Satan that prevent us from truly knowing God. He will explain the real problem regarding the infection of fear and selfishness within humankind, and reveal God's plan to heal and restore all to His original ideal."

Then Jesus made everything absolutely clear when He said, "I am He."

With joy in her heart, the woman ran to her village and told everyone the good news about the Savior. Satan was angry as the truth about God began to set hearts and minds free from his ancient lies.
(John 4:7-26)

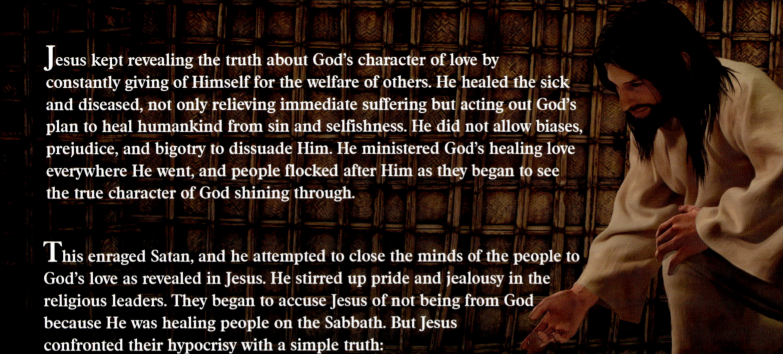

Jesus kept revealing the truth about God's character of love by constantly giving of Himself for the welfare of others. He healed the sick and diseased, not only relieving immediate suffering but acting out God's plan to heal humankind from sin and selfishness. He did not allow biases, prejudice, and bigotry to dissuade Him. He ministered God's healing love everywhere He went, and people flocked after Him as they began to see the true character of God shining through.

This enraged Satan, and he attempted to close the minds of the people to God's love as revealed in Jesus. He stirred up pride and jealousy in the religious leaders. They began to accuse Jesus of not being from God because He was healing people on the Sabbath. But Jesus confronted their hypocrisy with a simple truth: God is always working for our good, our healing, and our restoration.

Just like the Father, the Son is constantly working as well. The religious leaders were outraged and became even more determined to kill Jesus. However, He was not afraid. He continued to speak the truth in love. He told all who would listen that they didn't need to be afraid of the Father judging them. Instead, each person - by accepting or rejecting God - passes judgment on him- or herself. He made it clear that He had life in Him that was original, unborrowed, and underived. His life was the remedy to sin. His life was the cure to wickedness. Only by uniting with Him could sinners be healed. But the hearts of the religious leaders grew hard, and they would not listen. (John 5:1-27)

Despite the evidence of God's true character and His methods and principles being revealed so powerfully by Christ, Satan continued working to obstruct the understanding of the people. One day a group of individuals came to Jesus and asked, "What do we have to do in order to accomplish the work God requires of us so we can enjoy eternal life?"

Jesus answered, "God doesn't require that you perform some work or task to enjoy complete healing of mind and reconciliation with Him. All He requires of you is this: to believe the truth that I have come to reveal—which will result in the lies of Satan being expelled from your minds. This will restore your trust in God and bring powerful healing into your life so that you may live forever."

So they asked Him, "What miracle will you perform so that we may see it and trust you? What will you do to prove that you are not lying to us? Our forefathers ate manna in the desert just as it was written: 'He gave them bread from heaven to eat.'"

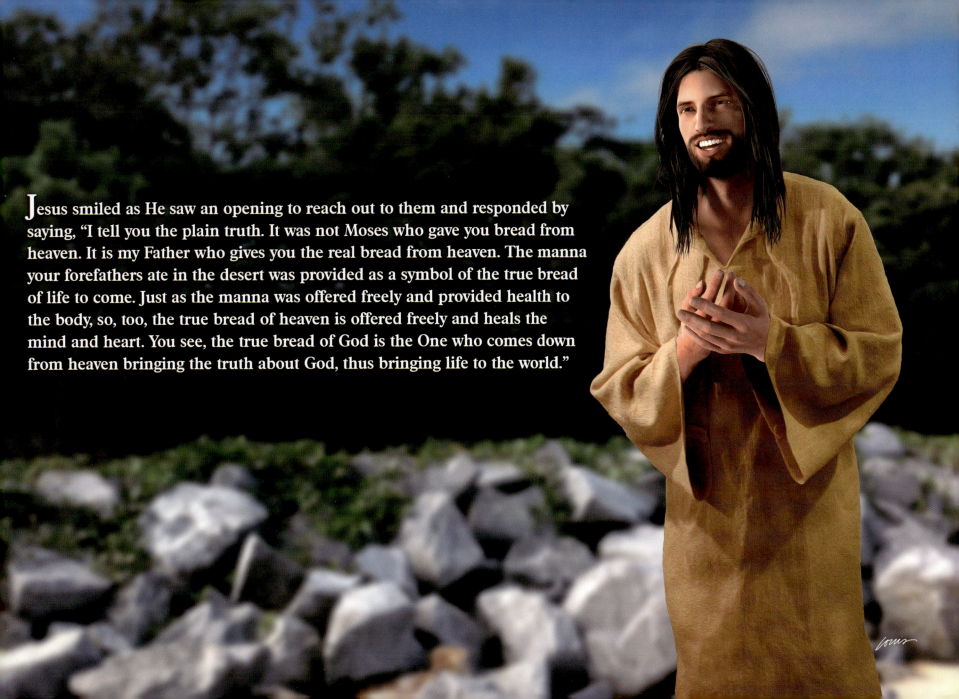

Jesus smiled as He saw an opening to reach out to them and responded by saying, "I tell you the plain truth. It was not Moses who gave you bread from heaven. It is my Father who gives you the real bread from heaven. The manna your forefathers ate in the desert was provided as a symbol of the true bread of life to come. Just as the manna was offered freely and provided health to the body, so, too, the true bread of heaven is offered freely and heals the mind and heart. You see, the true bread of God is the One who comes down from heaven bringing the truth about God, thus bringing life to the world."

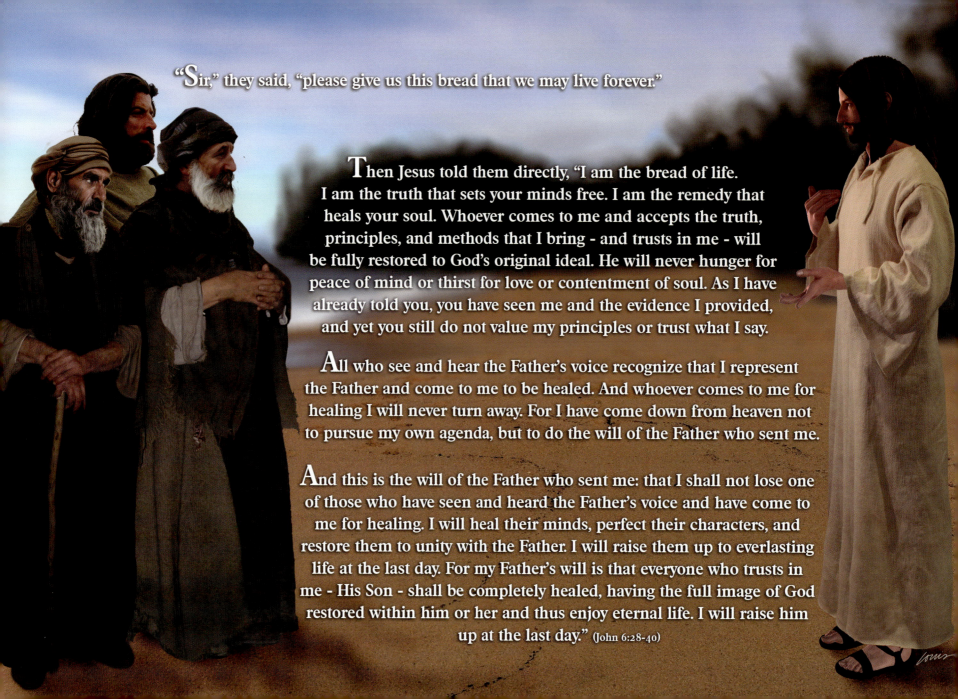

"Sir," they said, "please give us this bread that we may live forever."

Then Jesus told them directly, "I am the bread of life. I am the truth that sets your minds free. I am the remedy that heals your soul. Whoever comes to me and accepts the truth, principles, and methods that I bring - and trusts in me - will be fully restored to God's original ideal. He will never hunger for peace of mind or thirst for love or contentment of soul. As I have already told you, you have seen me and the evidence I provided, and yet you still do not value my principles or trust what I say.

All who see and hear the Father's voice recognize that I represent the Father and come to me to be healed. And whoever comes to me for healing I will never turn away. For I have come down from heaven not to pursue my own agenda, but to do the will of the Father who sent me.

And this is the will of the Father who sent me: that I shall not lose one of those who have seen and heard the Father's voice and have come to me for healing. I will heal their minds, perfect their characters, and restore them to unity with the Father. I will raise them up to everlasting life at the last day. For my Father's will is that everyone who trusts in me - His Son - shall be completely healed, having the full image of God restored within him or her and thus enjoy eternal life. I will raise him up at the last day." (John 6:28-40)

Chapter Sixteen - Healing

We Watchers noticed that one particular day, Satan became extra furious at Jesus. God's Son was in the Temple teaching a crowd of people, so Satan inspired the lawyers and Pharisees to try and catch Him off guard. First, these evil men entrapped a woman into adultery and then dragged her down the street and threw her down at Jesus' feet. Then they slyly said, "What should be done with her? The law of Moses says we should stone her to death. What do you say?" They thought they had Jesus cornered. If Jesus said, "Let her go," they would accuse Him before the people of undermining the law of Moses. But if He said to stone her, they would report Him to the Romans as someone ignoring their authority, because only the Romans could inflict the death penalty.

Jesus was not deceived by their trickery. He calmly bent down and used His finger to write in the sand. Slowly, carefully, He revealed the various sins that those who brought the woman had committed. He wrote just the sins - no names or details. As the men persisted that Jesus give an answer, He stood up and said, "Whichever of you is without sin, let him be the one to cast the first stone." Then He bent down and wrote more of their sins in the sand.

At this point, those who heard what He said and saw what He was writing cleared their throats and quietly slipped away. Finally, only Jesus and the woman were left standing alone. Then Jesus said gently to her, "Dear woman, where are all those who brought you here? Has no one condemned you?"

"No one, sir," she said.

"I don't condemn you either," Jesus told her. "Now go and live free from your past mistakes."

When Jesus again spoke to the people, He stated, "I am the true light revealing God's character, principles, and methods to the world. Whoever prefers what I am revealing and opens his or her mind to understanding this truth will no longer walk in the darkness of Satan's ways or live in fear of God because of Satan's lies. Instead, they will have the truth that brings eternal life." (John 8:1-12)

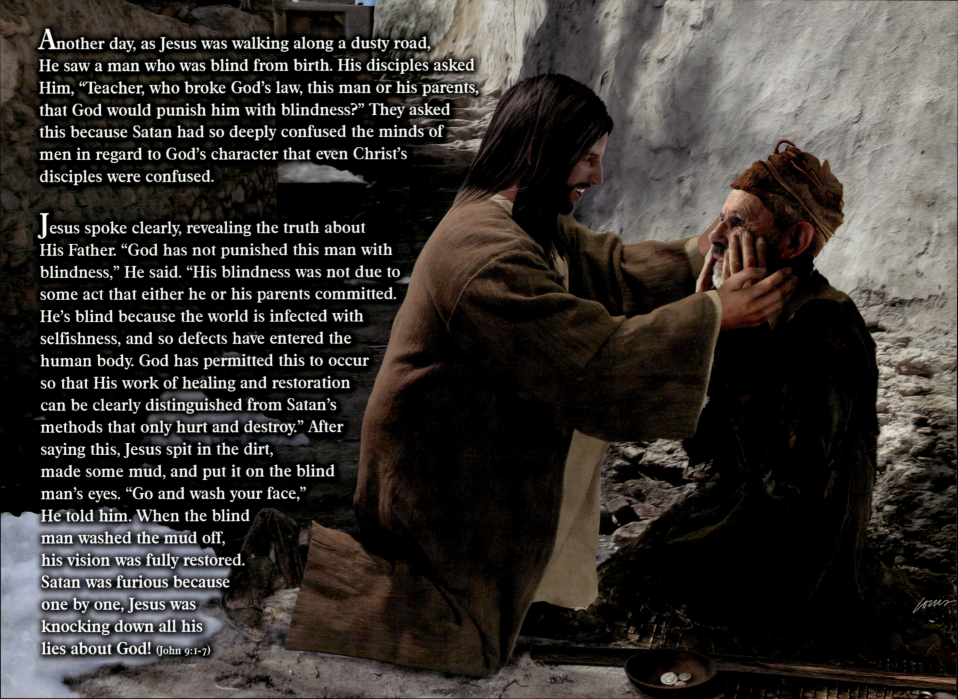

Another day, as Jesus was walking along a dusty road, He saw a man who was blind from birth. His disciples asked Him, "Teacher, who broke God's law, this man or his parents, that God would punish him with blindness?" They asked this because Satan had so deeply confused the minds of men in regard to God's character that even Christ's disciples were confused.

Jesus spoke clearly, revealing the truth about His Father. "God has not punished this man with blindness," He said. "His blindness was not due to some act that either he or his parents committed. He's blind because the world is infected with selfishness, and so defects have entered the human body. God has permitted this to occur so that His work of healing and restoration can be clearly distinguished from Satan's methods that only hurt and destroy." After saying this, Jesus spit in the dirt, made some mud, and put it on the blind man's eyes. "Go and wash your face," He told him. When the blind man washed the mud off, his vision was fully restored. Satan was furious because one by one, Jesus was knocking down all his lies about God! (John 9:1-7)

Chapter Seventeen - Truth Revealed

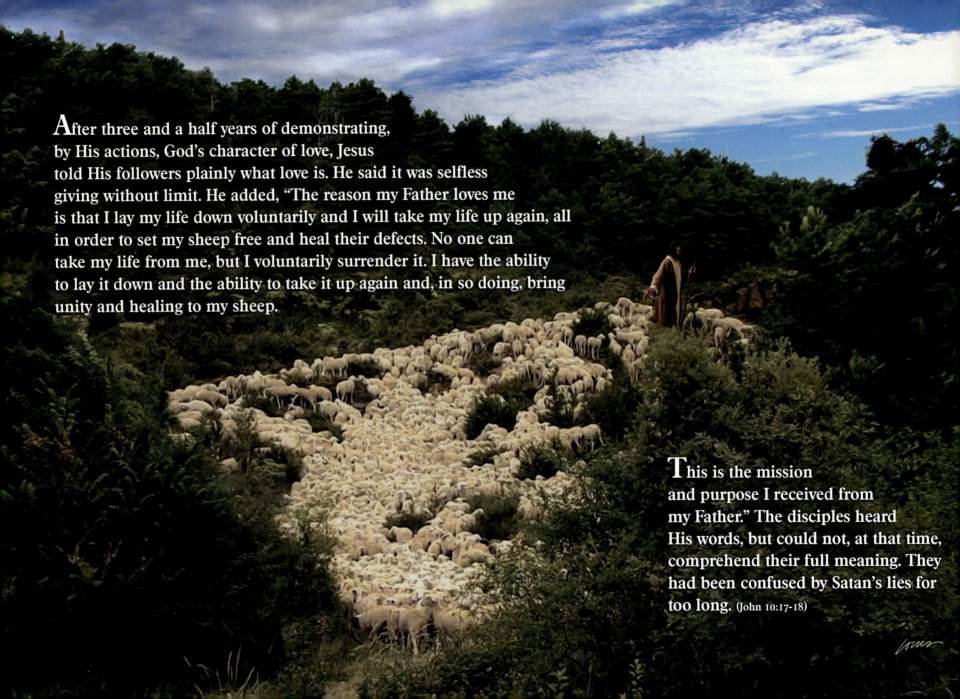

After three and a half years of demonstrating, by His actions, God's character of love, Jesus told His followers plainly what love is. He said it was selfless giving without limit. He added, "The reason my Father loves me is that I lay my life down voluntarily and I will take my life up again, all in order to set my sheep free and heal their defects. No one can take my life from me, but I voluntarily surrender it. I have the ability to lay it down and the ability to take it up again and, in so doing, bring unity and healing to my sheep.

This is the mission and purpose I received from my Father." The disciples heard His words, but could not, at that time, comprehend their full meaning. They had been confused by Satan's lies for too long. (John 10:17-18)

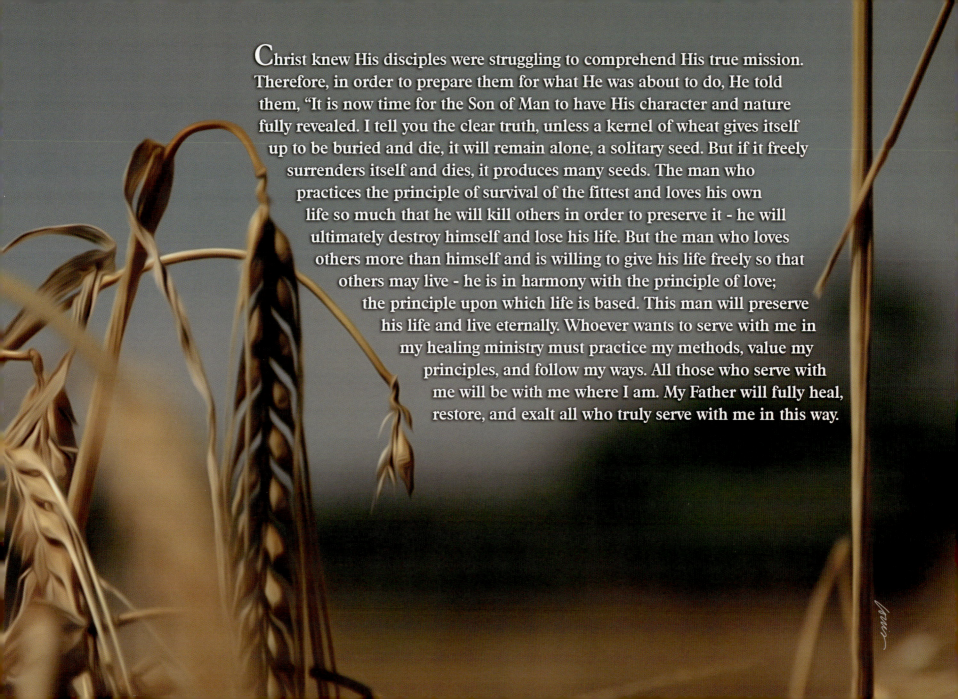

Christ knew His disciples were struggling to comprehend His true mission. Therefore, in order to prepare them for what He was about to do, He told them, "It is now time for the Son of Man to have His character and nature fully revealed. I tell you the clear truth, unless a kernel of wheat gives itself up to be buried and die, it will remain alone, a solitary seed. But if it freely surrenders itself and dies, it produces many seeds. The man who practices the principle of survival of the fittest and loves his own life so much that he will kill others in order to preserve it - he will ultimately destroy himself and lose his life. But the man who loves others more than himself and is willing to give his life freely so that others may live - he is in harmony with the principle of love; the principle upon which life is based. This man will preserve his life and live eternally. Whoever wants to serve with me in my healing ministry must practice my methods, value my principles, and follow my ways. All those who serve with me will be with me where I am. My Father will fully heal, restore, and exalt all who truly serve with me in this way.

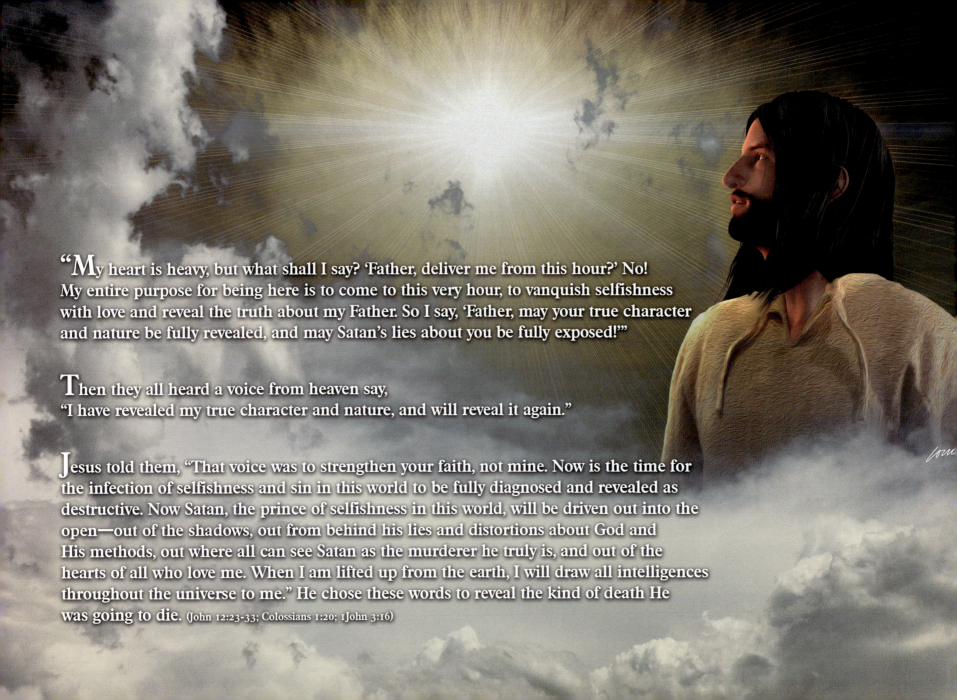

"My heart is heavy, but what shall I say? 'Father, deliver me from this hour?' No! My entire purpose for being here is to come to this very hour, to vanquish selfishness with love and reveal the truth about my Father. So I say, 'Father, may your true character and nature be fully revealed, and may Satan's lies about you be fully exposed!'"

Then they all heard a voice from heaven say, "I have revealed my true character and nature, and will reveal it again."

Jesus told them, "That voice was to strengthen your faith, not mine. Now is the time for the infection of selfishness and sin in this world to be fully diagnosed and revealed as destructive. Now Satan, the prince of selfishness in this world, will be driven out into the open—out of the shadows, out from behind his lies and distortions about God and His methods, out where all can see Satan as the murderer he truly is, and out of the hearts of all who love me. When I am lifted up from the earth, I will draw all intelligences throughout the universe to me." He chose these words to reveal the kind of death He was going to die. (John 12:23-33; Colossians 1:20; 1John 3:16)

Chapter Eighteen - Supper

On Thursday before Passover, supper was being served to Jesus and His disciples. Simon's son Judas Iscariot had already decided to follow the devil's suggestion and betray Jesus. Jesus, having received all power from His Father, got up from His meal, took off His outer garment, and wrapped a towel around His waist. Then He poured water in a bowl and began to wash the dirty feet of His disciples, drying them with the towel around His waist. It was a beautiful illustration of how God uses His power to cleanse, heal, and restore. Satan was livid as Jesus demonstrated that all He had said about God was an outright lie. (John 13:1-5)

Jesus knew Satan had filled His disciples' minds with all kinds of distortions about God, so after washing their feet He said, "Don't let fear and doubt trouble your hearts. Put your full trust in God, and trust me also. In my Father's home there is room for all who want to be there. If this were not true, I would tell you. I am going there to direct all the agencies in heaven in preparing for your future arrival. And if I go and prepare all things for you, I will return and take everyone who has been brought back into unity with the principles of heaven to be there with me, so that we may all be together. You now know the place where I am going."

One of the twelve, Thomas, expressed what the others thought: "But Lord, we don't know where you are going or how to get there. How can we know the way?"

Jesus answered gently,

"I am the way back to my Father. I am the truth revealing my Father's character and the principles upon which life is based. I am the source of all life. I am the bridge, and no one comes to the Father except through me. From now on, you know Him and have seen Him, for I am the full and complete revelation of the Father in human flesh."

Jesus answered patiently, "Don't you know me, Philip, even after all I have said and done among you these years together? Anyone who has seen me has seen the Father. Don't you understand? I am an exact representation of Him! So how can you say, 'Show us the Father'? Don't you believe that I am in complete unity with the Father, that we are the same in mind, heart, attitude, character, method, disposition, principle, and will? Don't you believe that the Father is with me? The words I speak are not my own ideas or methods but are the exact thoughts of my Father whose character and principles live in me. His work is being carried out through me. You must believe when I tell you that I am in complete unity in every way with my Father, and He is in complete unity in every way with me. Or at least believe all the evidence I have provided revealing that truth. Anyone who genuinely trusts me will also be in unity with the Father and reveal His character just as I have. His life will be a further revelation of the life-giving power of God and the healing strength of His methods. My life reveals the truth of God's character and methods, but those who trust in me will not only reveal God's methods, but they will also show that His methods, when applied in trust via the Spirit, actually heal and transform those deformed by sin. Even though I am going to the Father, I will do whatever you ask that is in harmony with my character, methods, and principles so that I may bring honor and glory to the Father by revealing the healing and life-giving power of His methods. You may ask me for anything in harmony with my character and methods and I will do it

"If you love me, you will practice all my methods and principles because you understand, agree with, and prefer my ways. And the Father and I will give you another Helper to be with you forever - the Spirit of truth - who will enlighten your minds to comprehend the truth. Those who prefer the methods of this world - the methods of deceit - cannot accept the Spirit because they, having rejected truth, don't recognize or know Him. But you will know Him, for you know me, and He represents all that I am. He will establish my character, methods, and principles within you. I will not abandon you and leave you as orphans; I will come to you." (John 14:1-18)

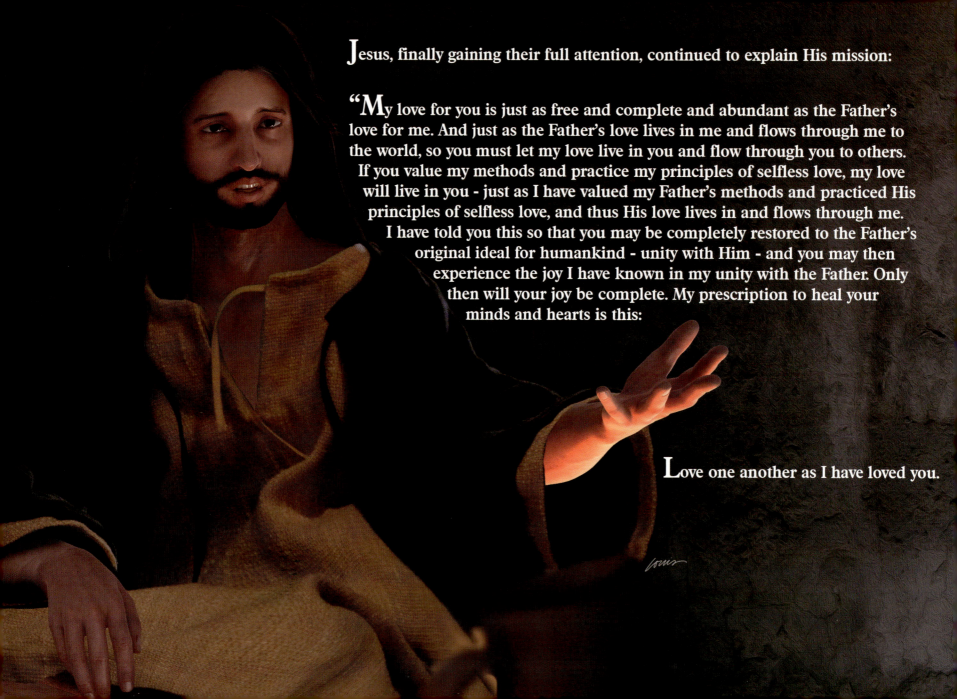

Jesus, finally gaining their full attention, continued to explain His mission:

"My love for you is just as free and complete and abundant as the Father's love for me. And just as the Father's love lives in me and flows through me to the world, so you must let my love live in you and flow through you to others. If you value my methods and practice my principles of selfless love, my love will live in you - just as I have valued my Father's methods and practiced His principles of selfless love, and thus His love lives in and flows through me. I have told you this so that you may be completely restored to the Father's original ideal for humankind - unity with Him - and you may then experience the joy I have known in my unity with the Father. Only then will your joy be complete. My prescription to heal your minds and hearts is this:

Love one another as I have loved you.

There is no greater love than this:
that a man lay his life down to save his friends.

This is the principle of life,
the central principle of the
kingdom of God. This love is the
cure for the infection that is
destroying humankind.
The infection is Satan's wicked
disease of survival-of-the-fittest,
which loves self so much that
a man will kill his friends in
order to save himself. You
are my friends if you take
my prescription and love
one another.

I do not want you to be my
slaves, because slaves only do
what they are told. They don't
understand what the master is
doing or understand the master himself.
Their hearts are not in harmony with the master,
and what they do they don't do freely. I want you to be my friends,
to understand what I am doing and to freely choose to be in unity with me.
That is why I have told you everything the Father and I are trying to accomplish, so that your hearts
and minds will be in harmony with us. You did not come seeking me. I came seeking to heal and restore you, so that you
will develop a character in harmony with mine, a character that will not be shaken. Then the Father will give you whatever
you ask as you work in harmony with us to finish our mission. This is my prescription: Love one another." (John 15:9-17)

Because Satan had so filled the minds of people with distorted ideas about God, Jesus had to plainly tell His disciples the truth that there was no need for Him to pray to the Father on their behalf. He told them, "Thus far I have been speaking to you in figures of speech and symbolic language.

But now I will not use symbols and metaphor but tell you plainly about my Father. Then you can speak to the Father yourself. I will not need to speak to the Father for you, because He has always loved you. Now that you understand that I came to reveal the Father, you realize your love for me is also your love for the Father. I came from the Father and brought the truth about Him into the world. Now my mission here is almost complete. I am leaving this world and returning to the Father."

Jesus' disciples told Him, "Finally, you are speaking clearly and without symbols or metaphors. Now we understand that you do know all things; you even know what we are thinking before we ask any questions. You are able to know our thoughts before we tell you. This convinces us beyond any doubt that you came from God." (John 16:25-30)

After Jesus had told His disciples these things, He looked toward heaven and began talking with His Father. The disciples heard Him say, "Father, the time for the completion of my mission has come. Now bring the attention of the entire universe to me, that I may reveal your true nature, character, and government, thus bringing all glory and honor to you. For you placed the security of the entire universe in my hands, so that all who unite with me may have eternal life. I have exalted and magnified you on earth by completing the mission you gave me to do. I have revealed your true character, methods, and principles while exposing Satan as a liar and showing that his methods of selfishness are the cause of death. I've restored your law of love into humanity. Now, Father, bring me back to you, that I might occupy my rightful place at your side - the place I stood before this world was made." (John 17:1-5)

Chapter Nineteen - The Betrayal

When He had finished talking with His Father, Jesus and His disciples crossed the Kidron Valley. On the other side stood an olive grove that they often visited. (John 18:1)

Jesus knew that the final battle of His earthly mission was approaching. It would be the ultimate showdown between love and selfishness. He knew the outcome of this battle would determine the outcome of the entire universal war

Therefore, once Jesus and His disciples reached the Garden of Gethsemane, Jesus took Peter, James, and John farther into the garden and asked the others to remain behind and pray. He then said to the three with Him, "My heart is breaking. I am dying. Watch and pray with me."

Going a little farther alone, Jesus fell to the ground in anguish as He felt the full force of Satan's survival-of-the-fittest temptation - an overwhelming urge to abandon His mission and save Himself. The two opposing principles - God's law of selfless love and Satan's temptation to save self - warred with each other in His heart and mind. Satan was desperate. He used every ploy and deception at his disposal. Christ's human heart was breaking under the extreme stress.

Looking toward heaven, Christ prayed,

"Daddy, you can do anything. So please, if it is possible for any other way to be found, let me avoid this ordeal. But, Father, not as my feelings cry out. No, I choose to follow your plan and your will be done."

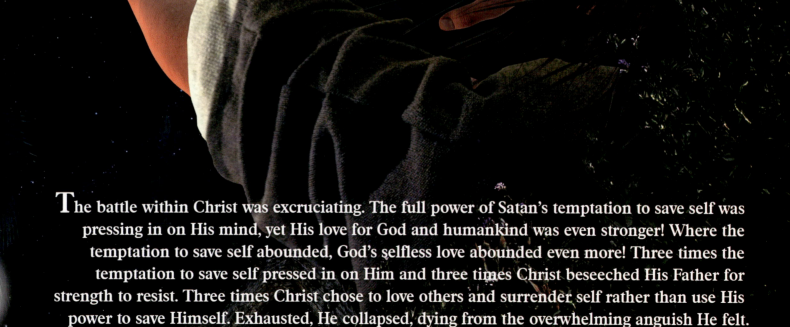

The battle within Christ was excruciating. The full power of Satan's temptation to save self was pressing in on His mind, yet His love for God and humankind was even stronger! Where the temptation to save self abounded, God's selfless love abounded even more! Three times the temptation to save self pressed in on Him and three times Christ beseeched His Father for strength to resist. Three times Christ chose to love others and surrender self rather than use His power to save Himself. Exhausted, He collapsed, dying from the overwhelming anguish He felt.

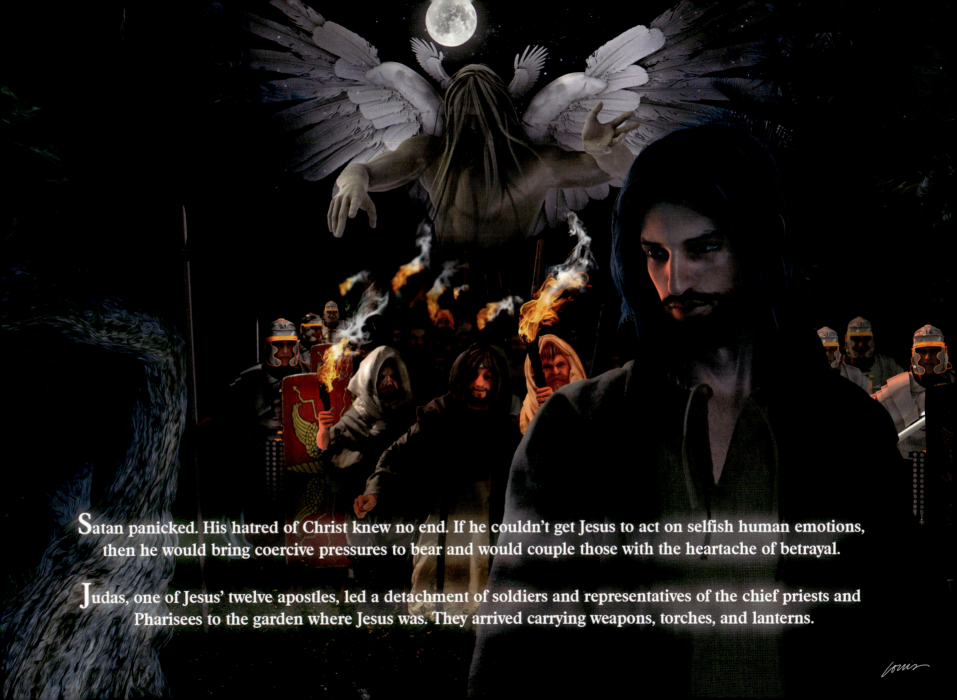

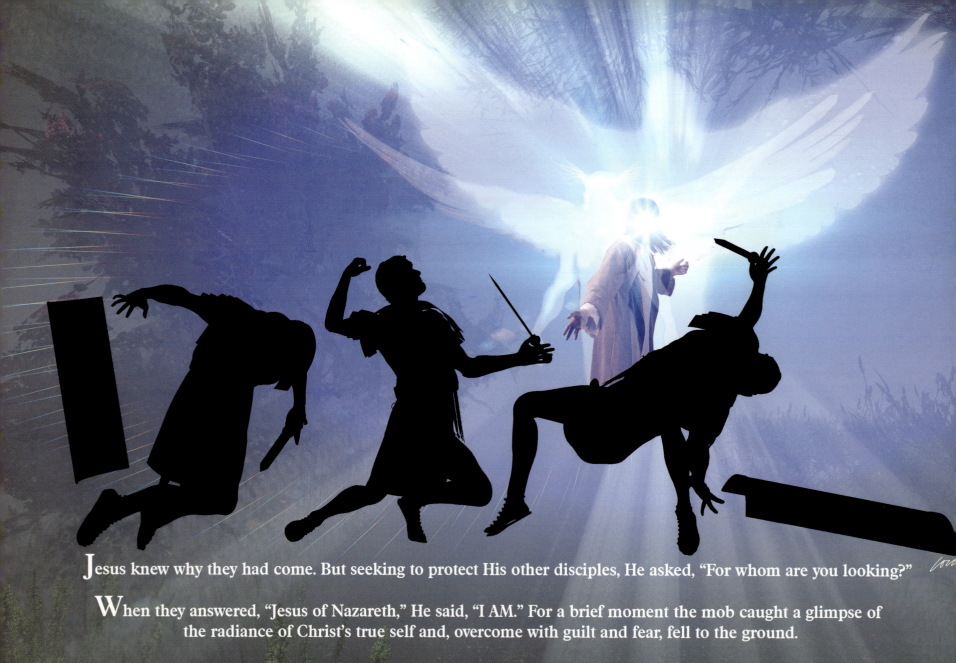

Simon Peter saw the soldiers fall and quickly drew his sword.

In one swift motion, he struck Malchus, the high priest's servant, severing his right ear.

That's when the soldiers, along with their commander and Jewish officials, revealed how damaging unhealed selfishness is to the mind and its ability to comprehend truth.

Despite the flash of Christ's true nature that knocked them to the ground, despite the observed miracle of Christ restoring Malchus' ear, despite Christ's loving action to protect them from Peter, they rejected the evidence and arrested Jesus.

They tied His hands and brought him to Annas, the former high priest, who was the father-in-law of that year's high priest, Caiaphas. (John 18:12-14)

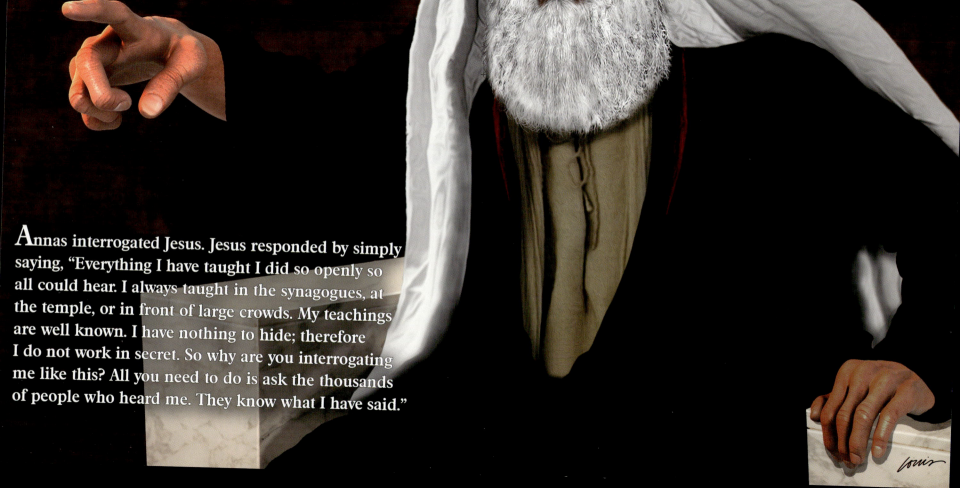

Annas interrogated Jesus. Jesus responded by simply saying, "Everything I have taught I did so openly so all could hear. I always taught in the synagogues, at the temple, or in front of large crowds. My teachings are well known. I have nothing to hide; therefore I do not work in secret. So why are you interrogating me like this? All you need to do is ask the thousands of people who heard me. They know what I have said."

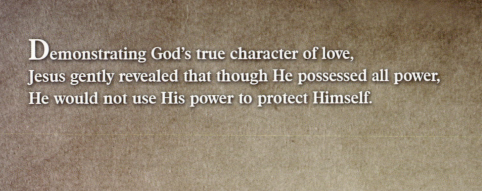

Demonstrating God's true character of love, Jesus gently revealed that though He possessed all power, He would not use His power to protect Himself.

He concluded by saying,

"If I said something wrong, show me what is wrong. But if I spoke the truth, why did you hit me?"

Satan couldn't believe what he was seeing. This is not possible, he thought. How can He stay so calm? But Jesus kept on loving others despite the abuse. So Annas, unable to get Jesus to stop loving perfectly, sent Jesus to Caiaphas the high priest. (John 18:20-24)

We Watchers, along with the angels in heaven watched with astonishment as God's chosen people - those blessed with Scripture, who for generations had observed the ceremonies that taught of Christ's mission of restoration and love - prepared to crucify their Creator. Amazingly, these same people refused to enter Pilate's palace because they didn't want to be ceremonially unclean. Unbelievably, they thought that they could actually keep the Passover while killing the very One to whom the Passover pointed. We began to realize that someone could outwardly observe all the commandments of God, yet still be God's enemy in his or her heart. We understood what Christ told Nicodemus: that humans needed a renewal of heart in order to have God's law of love restored within them.

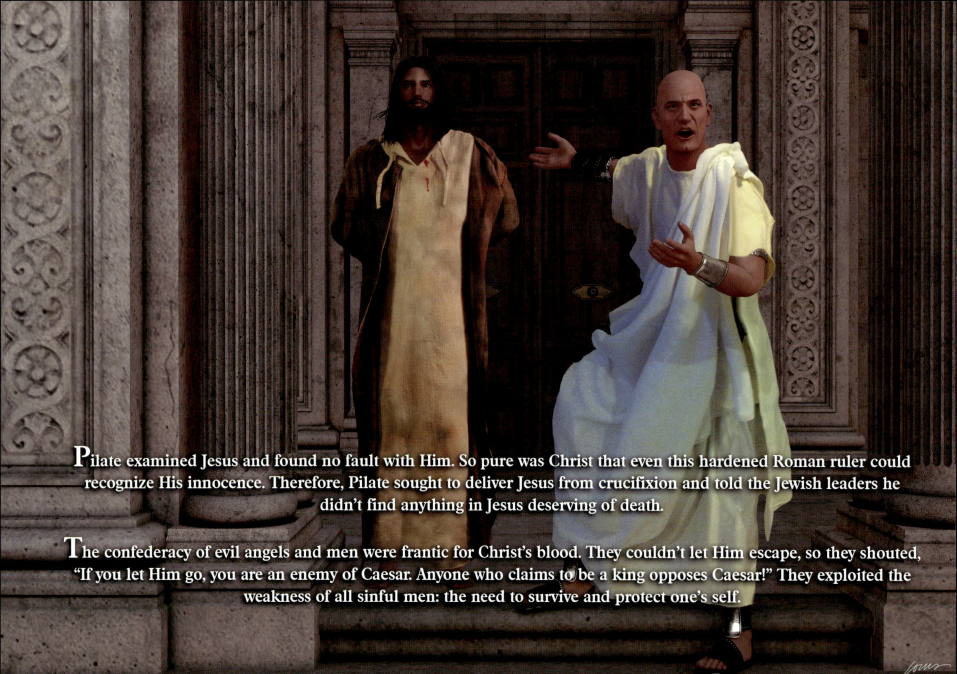

Pilate examined Jesus and found no fault with Him. So pure was Christ that even this hardened Roman ruler could recognize His innocence. Therefore, Pilate sought to deliver Jesus from crucifixion and told the Jewish leaders he didn't find anything in Jesus deserving of death.

The confederacy of evil angels and men were frantic for Christ's blood. They couldn't let Him escape, so they shouted, "If you let Him go, you are an enemy of Caesar. Anyone who claims to be a king opposes Caesar!" They exploited the weakness of all sinful men: the need to survive and protect one's self.

"Here is your king!"

When Pilate heard this, he became fearful for his own position and authority. So he had Jesus brought out to the people and then he sat down on his judgment seat. It was noon on the Friday before Passover. He shouted to the Jews,

Exhausted and frustrated, not knowing how to save Jesus and wanting to appease the Jews in order to secure his own position, Pilate's fear, insecurity, and drive to protect self took over his decision-making, and he sacrificed his principles. He reluctantly motioned to the guards and surrendered Jesus to be crucified. (John 18:28–19:16)

Chapter Twenty One - The Achievement

The angels in heaven were weeping, their hearts breaking. How could one of their own have become so hateful, so evil? How could human beings - created in the very image of God - become so cruel, so abusive, so hardened? They longed to step in and deliver Christ, but the Father restrained them, telling them to watch and learn. He understood that Satan and his true nature, character, and methods of selfishness must be fully exposed and that the true power of selfless love - the truth of God's character of love - must be fully revealed! Satan must be completely driven out of the affections of intelligent beings.

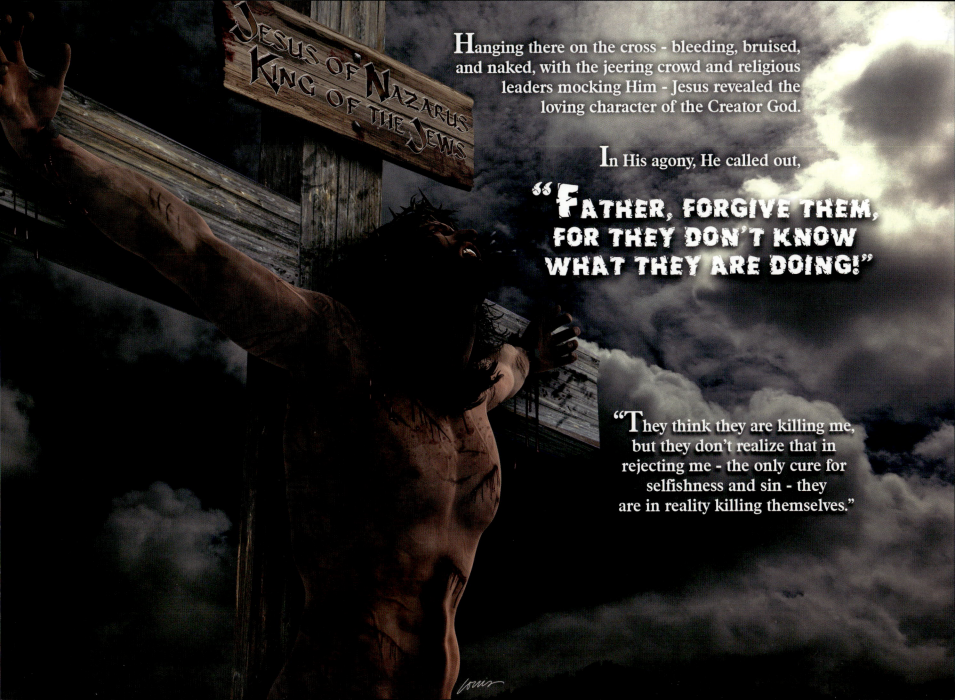

Hanging there on the cross - bleeding, bruised, and naked, with the jeering crowd and religious leaders mocking Him - Jesus revealed the loving character of the Creator God.

In His agony, He called out,

"Father, forgive them, for they don't know what they are doing!"

"They think they are killing me, but they don't realize that in rejecting me - the only cure for selfishness and sin - they are in reality killing themselves."

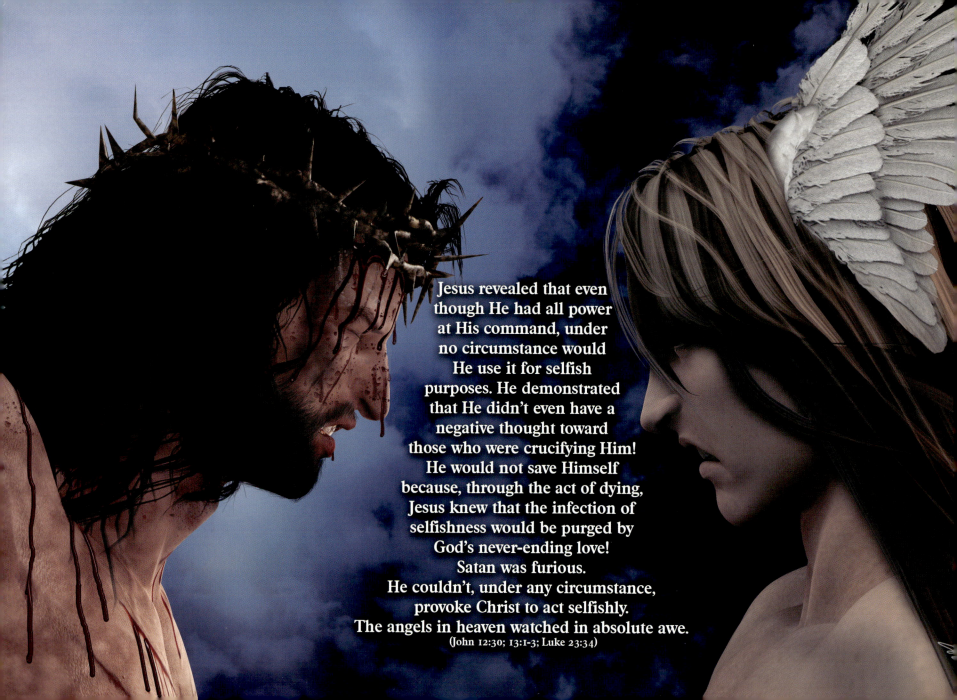

Jesus revealed that even though He had all power at His command, under no circumstance would He use it for selfish purposes. He demonstrated that He didn't even have a negative thought toward those who were crucifying Him! He would not save Himself because, through the act of dying, Jesus knew that the infection of selfishness would be purged by God's never-ending love! Satan was furious. He couldn't, under any circumstance, provoke Christ to act selfishly. The angels in heaven watched in absolute awe.
(John 12:30; 13:1-3; Luke 23:34)

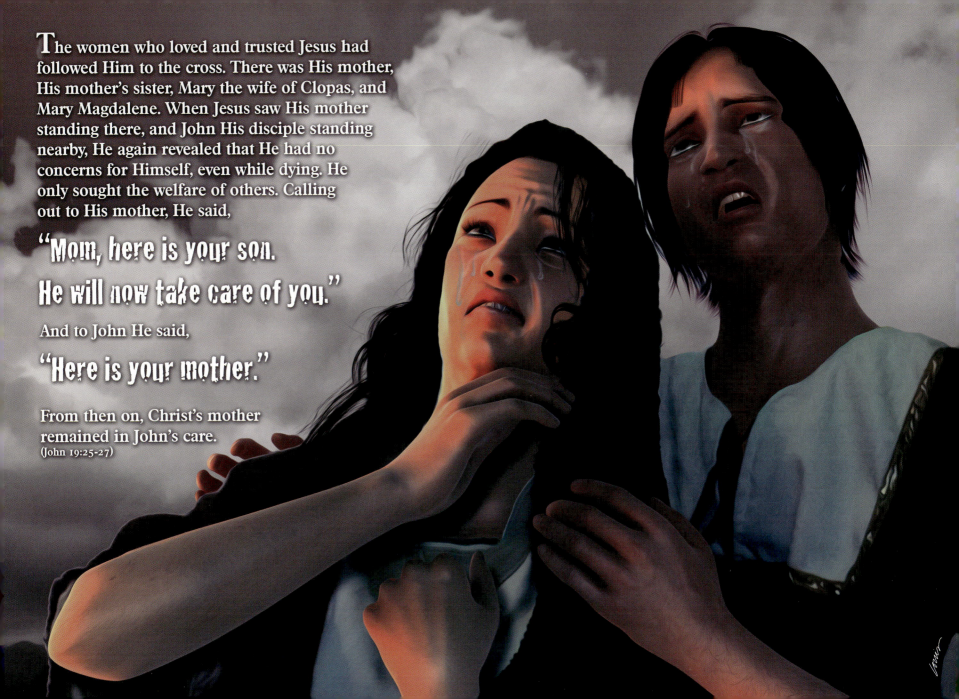

The women who loved and trusted Jesus had followed Him to the cross. There was His mother, His mother's sister, Mary the wife of Clopas, and Mary Magdalene. When Jesus saw His mother standing there, and John His disciple standing nearby, He again revealed that He had no concerns for Himself, even while dying. He only sought the welfare of others. Calling out to His mother, He said,

"Mom, here is your son. He will now take care of you."

And to John He said,

"Here is your mother."

From then on, Christ's mother remained in John's care.
(John 19:25-27)

People passing by the awful scene - influenced by satanic agencies - began to shout insults and ridicule Jesus, tempting Him to save Himself. "So you thought you could rebuild the temple in three days?" they shouted, laughing. "Then why don't you save yourself! Come on down if you are the Son of God!" The religious leaders and lawyers also tempted Him to rescue Himself, saying, "He saved others, but He can't save Himself! If He's the King of Israel then let Him come down from the cross. Come on, Jesus, save yourself if you want us to believe you!" Even one of the thieves crucified with Him also tempted Him in this way. But stronger than the temptation to save self was the power of God's love. In Christ's very humanity, while He was dying on the cross, love consumed selfishness. Christ chose love to the point of death rather than exercise His power to save self. Such love the universe had never seen. By choosing love at all costs, fallen humanity was cleansed of sin in the person of Jesus Christ. In the human nature of God's Son, love destroyed selfishness at the cross! (Matthew 27:39-44)

Jesus had accepted the mission of revealing the truth about God's character of love and exposing the true nature and character of sin. He had taken the responsibility of eradicating selfishness from humanity by consuming it with love. And He also, by "becoming sin though He knew no sin," revealed what God does to someone who refuses to be healed and reconciled to unity with Him. Jesus voluntarily laid down His life in absolute selfless love. He allowed Himself to be treated as if He were an unrepentant and un-healable sinner, thus revealing that sin severs the connection with God. God, who respects individual freedom to choose, lets sinners go; He gives them up to their own choice. Jesus revealed that God does not execute the sinner. It's sin that destroys. It's sin that separates the sinner from God. Jesus experienced the wrath of God poured out without mixture and felt the unity with His Father break apart. Feeling this separation, He cried out, "My God, my God, why have you forsaken me?"

(Matthew 27:46; Romans 1:18-28; 4:25; 6:23; 2 Corinthians 5:21; James 1:15)

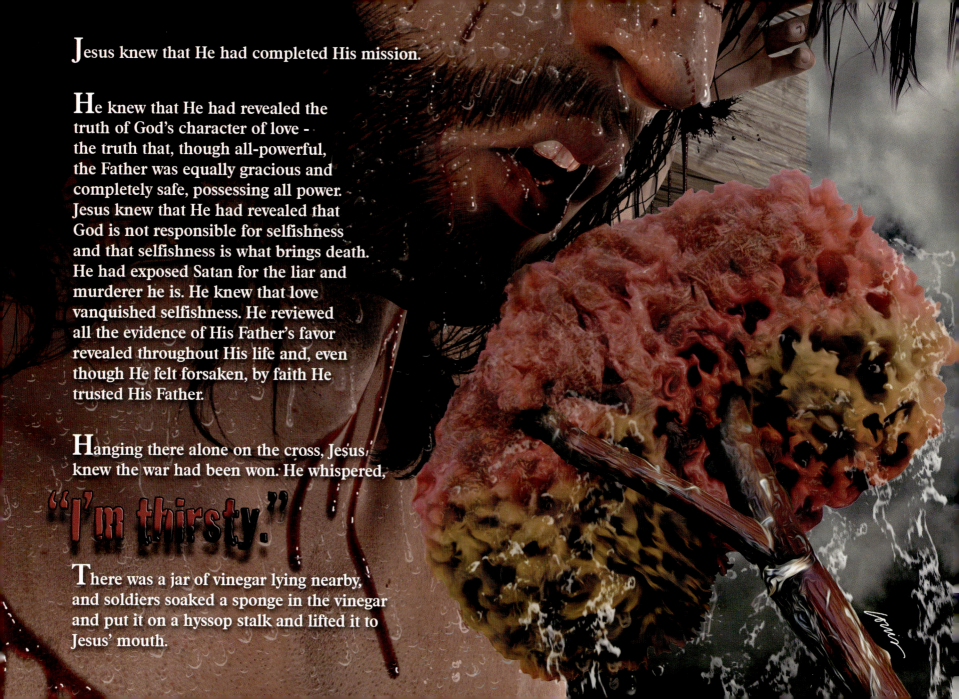

Jesus knew that He had completed His mission.

He knew that He had revealed the truth of God's character of love - the truth that, though all-powerful, the Father was equally gracious and completely safe, possessing all power. Jesus knew that He had revealed that God is not responsible for selfishness and that selfishness is what brings death. He had exposed Satan for the liar and murderer he is. He knew that love vanquished selfishness. He reviewed all the evidence of His Father's favor revealed throughout His life and, even though He felt forsaken, by faith He trusted His Father.

Hanging there alone on the cross, Jesus knew the war had been won. He whispered,

"I'm thirsty."

There was a jar of vinegar lying nearby, and soldiers soaked a sponge in the vinegar and put it on a hyssop stalk and lifted it to Jesus' mouth.

When He had moistened His lips, He called out in a clear voice,

"It is finished. Father, into your hands I commit my spirit."

With that, He bowed His head and breathed His last. He had completed His mission. He had finished the work given Him to do. He had vanquished selfishness through love and made the truth known. The onlooking universe was silenced. Never had they conceived of such selfless, absolute, perfect love. At that moment, all of Satan's lies about God were refuted. The universe was secure!
(Luke 23:44; John 19:28-30; Colossians 1:20)

When Christ died, the curtain separating the holy place from the most holy place in the Temple was torn from top to bottom. The lies of Satan that had separated humanity from God were also torn away, and the truth stood fully revealed. A new and living pathway back to the Father was secured by Christ's sacrificial death. There was a great earthquake, and rocks split apart. Tombs burst open, and many holy people who were sleeping in the grave were resurrected to life. They came out of the tombs and went throughout Jerusalem witnessing to the healing power of Jesus.

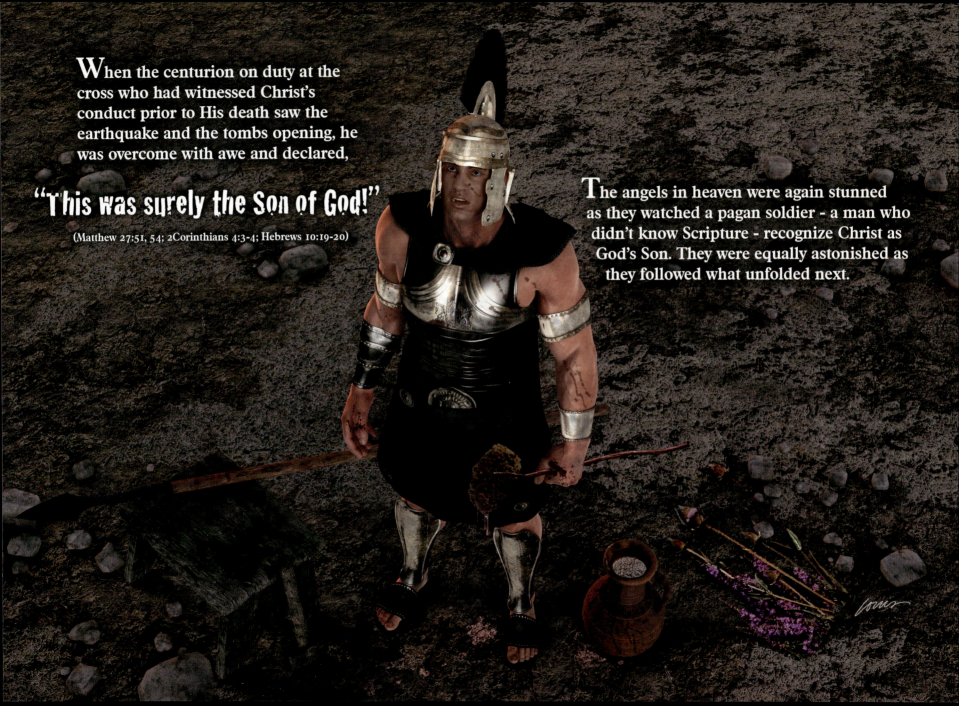

When the centurion on duty at the cross who had witnessed Christ's conduct prior to His death saw the earthquake and the tombs opening, he was overcome with awe and declared,

"This was surely the Son of God!"

(Matthew 27:51, 54; 2Corinthians 4:3-4; Hebrews 10:19-20)

The angels in heaven were again stunned as they watched a pagan soldier - a man who didn't know Scripture - recognize Christ as God's Son. They were equally astonished as they followed what unfolded next.

It was Friday, the Day of Preparation.

The next day was the special Sabbath of the Passover. The Jews, blessed with the Scriptures, prophetic guidance, feast days, the Temple services, the Sabbath commandment, and all the teaching tools that had led them to a knowledge of God, were so infected with Satan's lies that they petitioned Pilate to break the legs of those on the crosses so their bodies could be removed before Sabbath began.

Killing the Creator of the Sabbath, and then wanting Him off the cross in order to keep the Sabbath holy, represented astounding hypocrisy! The angels now realized how false god concepts damage the mind and destroy the character. Even when people observed the right regulations, if they retained false god concepts, they remained an enemy of God.

The angels realized that only the truth about God could set sinners free.
(John 8:32; 17:1-3;19:31-35; 2Corinthians 10:3-5)

Chapter Twenty Two - The Victory

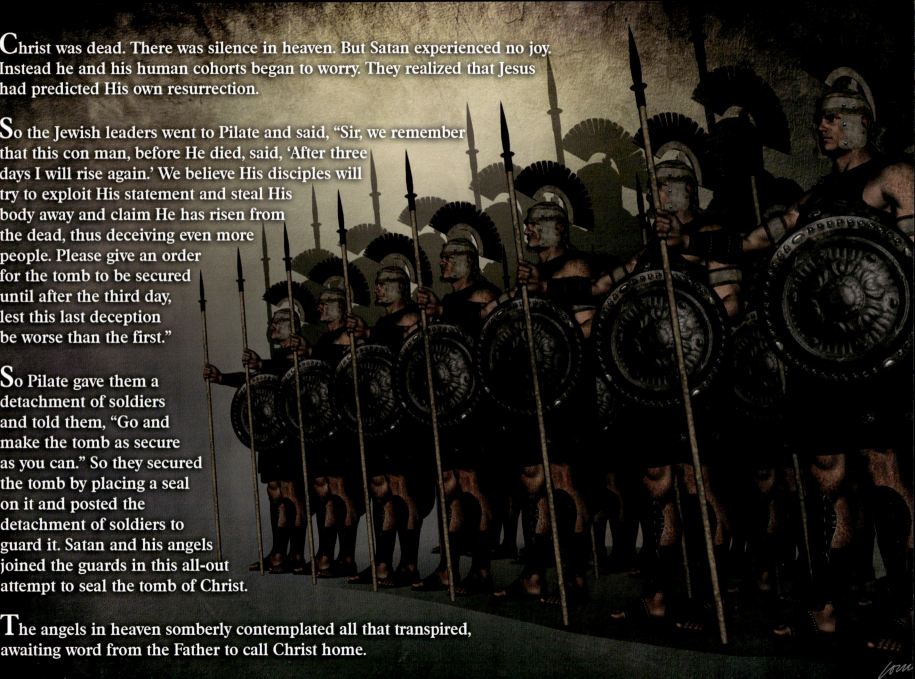

Christ was dead. There was silence in heaven. But Satan experienced no joy. Instead he and his human cohorts began to worry. They realized that Jesus had predicted His own resurrection.

So the Jewish leaders went to Pilate and said, "Sir, we remember that this con man, before He died, said, 'After three days I will rise again.' We believe His disciples will try to exploit His statement and steal His body away and claim He has risen from the dead, thus deceiving even more people. Please give an order for the tomb to be secured until after the third day, lest this last deception be worse than the first."

So Pilate gave them a detachment of soldiers and told them, "Go and make the tomb as secure as you can." So they secured the tomb by placing a seal on it and posted the detachment of soldiers to guard it. Satan and his angels joined the guards in this all-out attempt to seal the tomb of Christ.

The angels in heaven somberly contemplated all that transpired, awaiting word from the Father to call Christ home.

That word finally came! Early Sunday morning, an angel of the Lord came down from heaven with such great power that an earthquake shook the land and brilliant flashes of heavenly light pierced the air. His appearance was like lightning, and his clothes were whiter than snow. The soldiers were so afraid that their knees shook and they fell to the ground. Satan and his demonic host fled in terror as the heavenly angel made its approach.

The angel rolled away the stone, looked into the tomb, and declared with a loud voice, *"Your Father calls you home!"*

Jesus awoke from the dead. The moment His eyes fluttered open, the angels in heaven rejoiced. They shouted and sang songs of joy, and hallelujahs resounded throughout the universe. The Son of God lives!

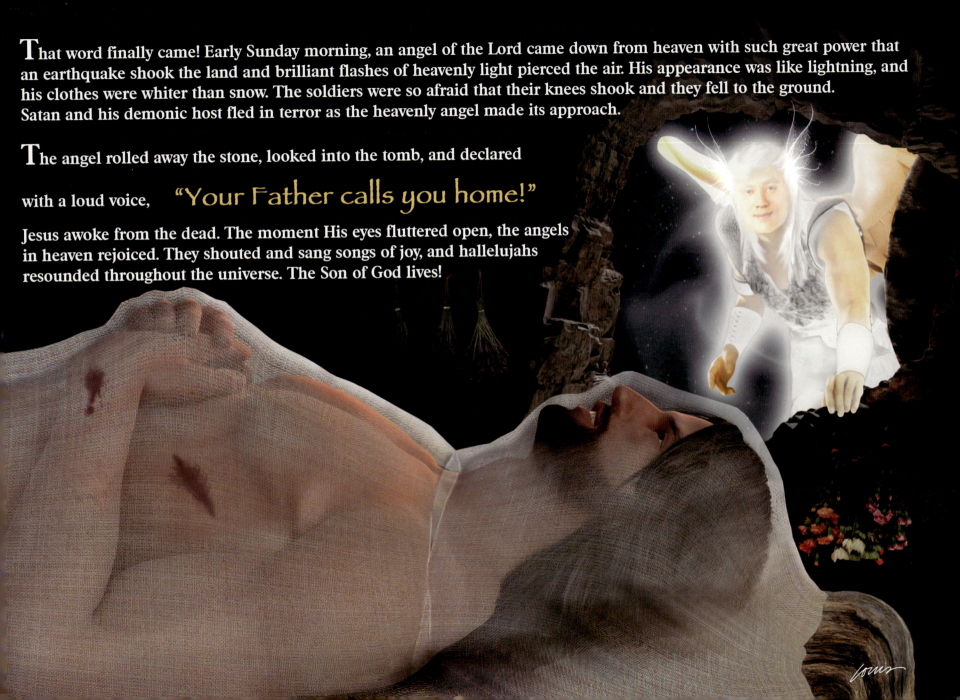

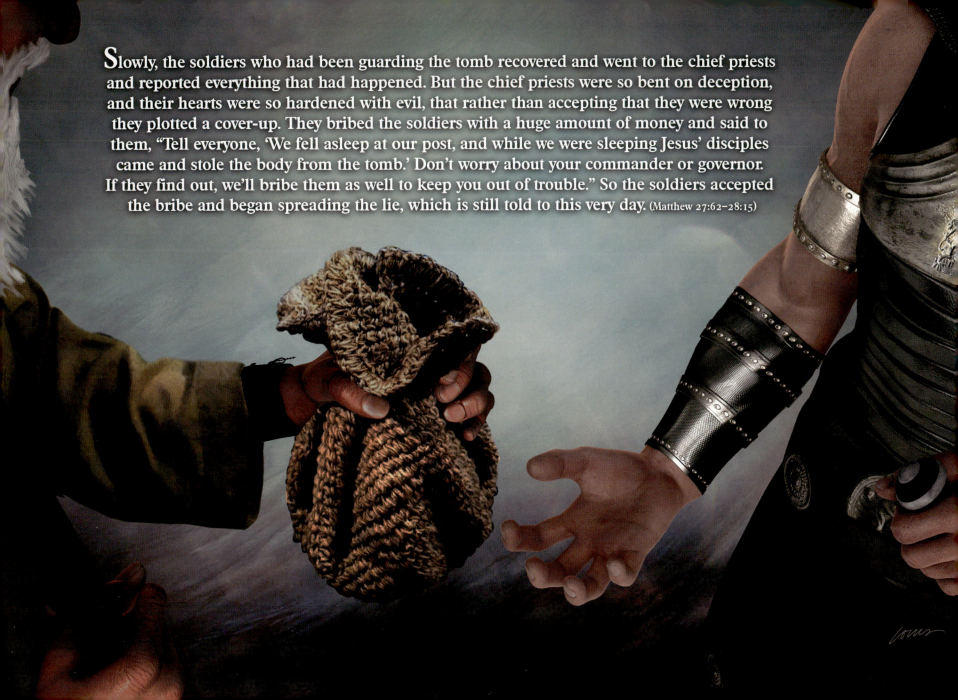

Slowly, the soldiers who had been guarding the tomb recovered and went to the chief priests and reported everything that had happened. But the chief priests were so bent on deception, and their hearts were so hardened with evil, that rather than accepting that they were wrong they plotted a cover-up. They bribed the soldiers with a huge amount of money and said to them, "Tell everyone, 'We fell asleep at our post, and while we were sleeping Jesus' disciples came and stole the body from the tomb.' Don't worry about your commander or governor. If they find out, we'll bribe them as well to keep you out of trouble." So the soldiers accepted the bribe and began spreading the lie, which is still told to this very day. (Matthew 27:62–28:15)

Chapter Twenty Three - The Future End

Days before the crucifixion, the disciples had wondered when the war between good and evil would finally be over, so they came to Jesus and asked, "Please tell us, when will you return to earth and bring a complete end to sin, selfishness, disease, and death?"

Jesus answered, "When this remedy - the good news of the truth about my Father, His methods, principles and character that refutes the lies of Satan, restores trust in me, and expels selfishness from the heart - is taken to the entire world, then the war will come to an end and I will return." He said, "At that time I will appear in the sky surrounded by clouds of brilliant angels, and there will be great power and glory. There will be a loud trumpet call, and the angels will gather from all over the earth everyone who has accepted the remedy and been healed."

(Matthew 24:3-31)

Satan sought to set himself up in God's spirit temple, the heart and mind of human beings, by convincing humans to worship a distorted concept of God. Satan sought to replace the truth that God is like Jesus - a Being of consummate love, grace, forgiveness, and beneficence - with the lie that God is a stern, judgmental, arbitrary, punitive being who requires appeasement of His wrath. He sought to infect Christianity with pagan ideas concerning the nature and character of God. And as the world accepted Satan's version, it slowly sank into an age of darkness. In the name of Christ, wars were waged, persecution flourished, and violent inquisitions and executions took place. Satan rejoiced as God was, once again, misrepresented as abusive, intolerant, and unreasonable. (Daniel 7; 2 Thessalonians 2:3-4; 1Peter 5:8; Revelation 12–13

- Lies believed results in broken love and trust.
- Broken love and trust results in fear and selfishness.
- Fear and selfishness results in destructive behaviors of self-preservation.
- Self-preservation results in guilt, shame, and damage to character, mind, and body, a terminal condition.

In reaction to this twisted, ugly, repressive idea of God, men began to question the idea of God altogether.

Peter prophesied that scoffers and doubters would arise; those who prefer the sickness of selfishness while ridiculing the cure, labeling the infection of selfishness as "normal." They would say, "Survival-of-the-fittest is the way the universe runs. We are here because of this law, not because of divine creation. Where is this so-called God? Where is the 'coming' He promised? Ever since human history has been recorded, the principles of evolution have governed life and all things continue just as they always have."

These scoffers deny the truth and overlook important facts. They fail to realize the true nature of God's kingdom of love. They don't understand that the Lord lives outside the constraints of time, and with Him a day is like a thousand years, and a thousand years is like a day. There is no delay on His part in keeping His promise to return.

He is simply waiting for what He has always been waiting for - the remedy to be taken to the entire world so that none who remain curable will be lost. (2 Peter 3:3-9)

We Watchers, who have observed all that has happened throughout history, have no doubt concerning what the future holds. Once the truth about God - as revealed by Jesus - is taken to the entire world so that all who are willing can be cured, the end will come. Jesus will appear in the fullness of His unveiled glory. Like lightning flashing across the sky, the fire of His beautiful presence will flow freely on the earth once again. The fire of unveiled holiness, pure truth, and love will consume sin, selfishness, and all disease. Every defect will be destroyed. Those who have rejected love and truth, who have preferred lies and selfishness, will be tormented by the reality of their unhealed condition as this unveiled inferno of love and truth burns freely. They won't want to look into the face of Christ. Instead, they'll run away, begging for the mountains to hide them. Then, there will be a loud roar and the sky will disappear. The very elements will melt in the intense heat, and the entire planet will be laid bare. All sin, all evil, all selfishness will vanish forever.

You ask, "Since the end will come in this way, what should be done?"

Our answer is simple.

Each man, each woman, and each child must partake of the cure of God's love that is found in Christ, and be healed. You can then spread the remedy to everyone you find.

On that day, the Lord will appear in the sky, accompanied by millions of angels, and will loudly command those sleeping in the graves - those who have previously taken the cure and been healed - to arise to everlasting life.

The trumpet call of victory will resound throughout the earth, and all those alive on the earth - who have also accepted the cure and been healed - will be taken up with those resurrected from the graves to meet Jesus in the air!

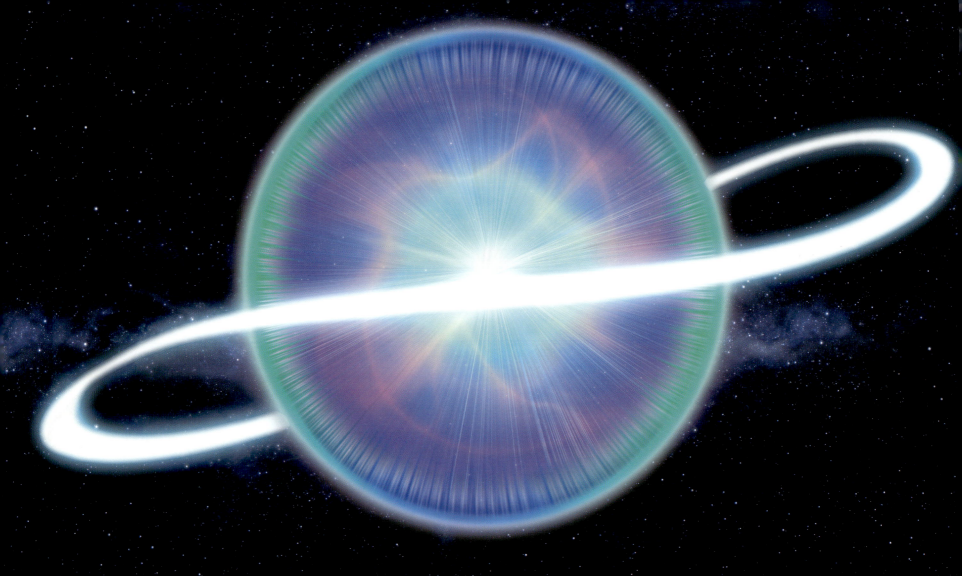

Then, after all sin and selfishness has been consumed and all disease and defect has been destroyed, Jesus will make a new atmosphere and an entirely new earth free from disease and defect, free from the infection of selfishness, free from the destructive principle of survival-of-the-fittest.

"Soon the long struggle will end. So use this journal wisely. Embrace the truth about God and His methods of Love. See past the business of each day to the reality of the cosmic conflict raging all around between love and fear, giving and taking. As we continue to observe the final events on planet earth, we hope you will partake of the remedy, choose the truth as revealed in Jesus, live to give, and unite yourself with the universe of love. Stay strong and don't give up, for the war is almost over!"

Timothy R. Jennings, M.D. is a Christian psychiatrist, author, international speaker, radio and TV personality, and has a private practice in Chattanooga, Tennessee. Dr. Jennings obtained his M.D. degree in 1990 from the University Of Tennessee College Of Medicine in Memphis, Tennessee and completed psychiatric residency at D.D. Eisenhower Army Medical Center in Augusta, Georgia. He served as the Division Psychiatrist for the 3rd Infantry division and is board certified in psychiatry by the American Board of Psychiatry and Neurology, a Master Psychopharmacologist, Adjunct Faculty at the UT College of Medicine Chattanooga campus, President-Elect of the Tennessee Psychiatric Association, Fellow of the American Psychiatric Association, Chairman of the Board of Regents of the Southern Psychiatric Association and is licensed to practice medicine in Tennessee, Georgia and Washington. Dr. Jennings was named one of America's Top Psychiatrists by the Consumer Research Institute of America in 2008, 2010, 2011 and 2012. He has two books in Publication, Could It Be This Simple?: A Biblical Model for Healing the Mind (Autumn House 2007, 2nd Edition Lennox Publishing 2012) and The God-Shaped Brain: How Changing Your View of God Transforms Your Life (IVP 2013).

Louis Johnson is currently a freelancer with a background in design, illustration, sculpting, and architecture. Louis launched his career as a graphic designer at Loma Linda University Medical Center, California. His works there included technical illustrations for the Journal of American Medical Association (JAMA), illustrations for the advancement of the Lithotripsy and graphics for medical exhibitions. He also sculpted a bronze portrait of philanthropist Irwin Schumann located in the Loma Linda University Medical Center's Schumann Pavilion. In 1986, he began working for several awards winning software companies such as, Cinemaware, Microillusions and New Tek. In 1992 he was principal artist for New World Computing "Might and Magic" series 3 & 4, then on to Mindscape as senior artist on "Tiger Wood's Golf" for EA Sports. In 1998, he moved from America to Australia and became art director for Torson Inc. designing the interface for the "Torson Strength and Flexibility Training System". In 2001, Louis joined Krome Studios as a senior graphic artist on the software version of "Jimmy Neutron, Boy Genius" and the movie "King Arthur". After retiring from the software industry, Louis taught illustration and graphic design at Qantm Digital and Media College. Since becoming a freelancer, his clients have included Brisbane City Council, Australian Aviation Workers in Army, Navy and Special Operations (Covert Aanti-Terrorist And Emergency Operations Unit), Outback Aviation Ministries, Connaught Engineering, and co-developed the book "Biomimetics: Nature Inspiring Innovation".